TRANSFORMING PEOPLE AND ORGANIZATIONS

TRANSFORMING PEOPLE AND ORGANIZATIONS

The Seven Steps of Spiritual Development

Margarete van den Brink

TEMPLE LODGE

Translated from Dutch by Ania Lentz-Michaelis

Temple Lodge Publishing
Hillside House, The Square
Forest Row, RH18 5ES

www.templelodge.com

Published by Temple Lodge 2004

Originally published in Dutch under the title *Spirituele ontwikkeling van mens en organisatie in zeven fasen* by Uitgeverij Ankh-Hermes bv, Deventer, Netherlands in 2002

A catalogue record for this book is available from the British Library

ISBN 1 902636 50 3

Cover by Andrew Morgan
Typeset by DP Photosetting, Aylesbury, Bucks.
Printed and bound by Cromwell Press Limited, Trowbridge, Wilts.

Contents

Foreword

We are not human beings having a spiritual experience;
we are spiritual beings having a human experience.
Teilhard de Chardin[i]

Writing this foreword offered me an opportunity to review the work my organization had started some years ago with the help of the author of this book and her approach to individual and organizational development. That work has given us new insights and new tools badly needed in a time of great turbulence and change. This book is written with the same clarity, forthrightness, sensitivity and spiritual insight I so appreciate in Margarete van den Brink's consultation work, and I am delighted to finally see the material elucidating her approach in print and available to a wider audience.

I cannot stress enough the timeliness of this book. In an era of progressive organizational dysfunction, intensifying conflict and alienation, and accelerating rates of change in social, economic and community life, all bringing with them a great increase in uncertainty and insecurity, it is important to locate the principles that drive and govern the evolutionary changes under way. 'While these are chaotic and turbulent times, they are hardly crazy ones. There is rhyme to both the reason and the unreason. Order lurks in the chaos; a deeper chaos still lurks in the order. Those who have eyes to see, ears to hear, and spirals in their minds to understand, will rest easier knowing the sky is not falling, after all' (Ronnie Lessem).[ii] The current instabilities and seeming breakdown of systems can be seen as a call for renewal and rebirth of organizations on a new plane and under a new paradigm. It may thus be important for an understanding of these trends to revisit the larger context of development of what we may loosely call 'the human project'.

This is what the author of this book sets out to do. She describes and aligns both the development of the individual and of organizations, showing that the same seven qualitative phase changes and corresponding processes are at work in both. It becomes clear that both, the changes in individuals, as well as those in organizations, societies and cultures, are the consequence of deep transformations of consciousness. The author first follows the development of the individual: from the infant's state of undivided unity to the child's embeddedness in the group; then to the adult's awakening, assertion, and possible catharsis of ego through crisis and transformation; on to the birth and development of the spiritual Self, the new ability for community; and finally to the possibility of a new, differentiated, conscious unity. She then explores gender differences and polarities on this trajectory, and relates her insights to relational processes. Finally the author guides us through the historic emergence of mankind, from clans to tribes, to nations, societies and cultures, and explores the organizational principles relevant to the various stages of consciousness. We soon come to see that in each developmental stage there are often echoes of earlier, transcended, now deficient, but not entirely defunct stages. There are also premonitions, partial and momentary anticipations of future stages, heralding further transformations. Human beings continuously forge new systems, new ways of seeing and new ways of living reality. However, although earlier cognitive systems can be transformed and transcended, they stay with us — just as more primitive modes of consciousness do. We thus, on the one hand, constantly enrich our arsenal of cognitive possibilities and widen our capacities of dialogue with the world; on the other we can, easily and at any time, regress into deficient modes.

For readers not familiar with the territory, it may be important to acknowledge that the book starts from several basic assumptions, or core principles:

- the assumption that there is a dynamic evolutionary principle at the heart of earthly and human existence, a continuous process of unfolding and evolutionary change
- the assumption that life on earth develops and undergoes progressive changes of consciousness, and that particular stages involved in this change are valid for individuals, organizations and societies alike
- the assumption, for the human context, of a development trajectory of continuous conscientization and individuation, a constant summons to 'become oneself', to increased awareness and understanding of the 'other' and, ultimately, to full realization of the interconnectedness, interdependence and higher unity of the multitude of diverse, individualized earthly manifestations
- and finally, the assumption that this development proceeds with the force of a natural law, and that thus both resistance or inability to move forward to higher modes of consciousness and concomitant processes of organization will inevitably lead to regression and breakdown

On this background the author then sheds light on the progressive development of conscious selfhood and the subsequent inversion of the relationship of the individual and the community. The quintessential development of humankind is the progressive release from divine guidance and primeval embeddedness in the community into moral and ethical independence and individuation. This evolutive process drives humankind out of all archaic, magical, mythical and eventually also mental contexts; it pushes us beyond ties of race, tribe, family, gender and culture into the final nakedness of isolated selfhood. It is accompanied by increasing loss of spiritual security and certainty. The metamorphosis of human consciousness, with its progress in intellectual rationality and increasing distance from the implicate origin, by necessity leads to increased ego-centredness and despiritualization of the world around us. Paradoxically, however, this loss is both the very prerequisite for and consequence of man's predisposition to freedom. Freedom, as we know, is the prerequisite for love—conscious, deep interest in the 'other'. 'We are true human beings only in so far as we are free. Without freedom, love is impossible' (Rudolf Steiner)[iii] and, 'love alone is capable of uniting living beings in such a way as to complete and fulfil them, for it alone takes them and joins them by what is deepest in themselves' (Teilhard de Chardin).[iv]

The described developments throw up the question: which social and organizational forms are appropriate for the different development stages of human beings? Margarete van den Brink explores this and argues that at our present stage in human development it is the task of *each individual* to renew the connection to the spiritual world, to consciously reintegrate him- or herself into the spiritual order of the universe. The inversion of the relationship of the individual to the community requires that, increasingly, the organization will have to put itself at the disposal of the development of the individual, so that in the future a new community of free and fully conscious human beings may arise. We consequently are now challenged to establish organizational forms that make it their prime task to support the unlocking of each individual's full human potential. This is a revolutionary change. It will only succeed if individual human beings will be able to move from self-centred egohood to true selfhood, to develop what Margarete here calls *the spiritual Self.*

The importance of this volume for me lies in the clarity and unambiguity with which it shows the core of each individual, the *Self*, to be the pivot for all future development. The author argues that regression into deficient phases and any feeling of comfort or acts of sentimental altruism this may elicit will not give us any ground to stand on, but that a spiritual future for humanity and the earth depends entirely on our ability to become fully conscious of this core 'self' and of the need to develop actively it's higher, self-transcending aspect, the *spiritual Self*. The latter is the real and only seat and fount of freedom, as this is where our individual spiritual essence is linked with the spiritual ground of the world. Only here will we, as individuals, be able to find the moral and ethical imaginations necessary for our continued survival. All other moral frameworks will dissolve. If, however, out of this source, we make, in total freedom, the *other* the centre of our loving interest, we will start the process of re-implicating the explicate world, and create what Teilhard de Chardin called the 'reign of love'. Love, in this context, is to be understood as the new principle of order in the world.

At the centre of the storm, the earthquake, the breakdown, is *the self*. The drama that unfolds is the drama of its motives and of its development to higher, more integrated stages. It is also the drama of responsibility for 'world development'. The scene is set initially by the thought structures we adhere to and by our resulting strategies and behavioural choices. These can be changed, but—at our present stage of development—only from *inside* the individual. Turbulence can lead to breakdown, it can also lead to breakthrough. The self is the eye of the needle, and change will only be able to enter through this gate. It is, says the author, the door to a new world.

I believe that, ultimately, all human beings share the same principal desires, to serve, to be safe, to be free, and to achieve this they want to be empowered, ensouled, inspired. I also believe that, implied in the desire to serve, which is arising in many human beings today, is what the more advanced stages described in this book envision: the striving for personal development, in order to enable and equip oneself to better 'contribute, in collaboration with others, to the development of the greater whole'.

The challenge for us now is how to get through the night of katabasis, the abyss, the ashes, the breakdown, to transformation and true metanoia. In practice: how do we handle questions of consensus versus instabilities, self-assertiveness versus group warmth, individual development versus organizational survival? The author shows us how, with the help of the reflection process, the development of the spiritual Self, and a deeper understanding of organizational processes appropriate for our time, we can successfully begin to work on this challenge.

I believe that we are engulfed in the birth pangs of a new age, an age in which the present angst may give way to new spiritual certainties. These, however, will be hard earned and earned individually. Yet, if experienced and realized by a critical mass of human beings, they could create new synergies, which may one day make the present world seem like the Dark Ages. 'The present moment finds our society attempting to negotiate the most difficult, but at the same time the most exciting, transition the human race has faced to date. It is not merely a transition to a new level of existence but the start of a new "movement" in the symphony of human history' (Clare Graves).ᵛ

If we accept the development trajectory of humankind as presented in this book, we can have confidence in the processes and suggested developments described here. This, in turn, can enable us to contribute towards a positive and viable future, notwithstanding phases of great turbulence and suffering. A larger picture arises, and we may learn to trust the thrust towards ever-increasing freedom and self-realization of the individual, fearless of what may appear as the breakdown of civil society. Insight into the path of human development and a deeper understanding of the human dynamics involved in this seemingly ubiquitous breakdown will help us to see the positive aspects, the aspects of growth in this process. It will aid us to recognize the nature and direction of the changes required from our organizations and ourselves. It will also help us accept the arduous task of self-development, and encourage us to not shy away from a bold recasting of the values and principles we may hold most dear. I am aware that with this task considerable odds are stacked against us. However, developing ourselves and our organizations in this way will be our greatest contribution to social sustainability and, ultimately, to world peace.

I wish this book all the success it deserves, and hope to see, in due course, a companion volume—a work book or field book—based on the phase model as presented here, focusing on skills, techniques and strategies required to further develop the spiritual dimensions for both individuals and organizations.

Tyll van de Voort[vi]

Introduction

In life one sometimes experiences and does all sorts of things, the meaning of which one only later understands. This happened in my own life.

After my studies, I first worked as a counsellor for individuals. Through this, I was asked by companies to support employees who were having problems in their mutual relationships and collaboration. This in turn led to my present work: support of organizations in their process of change and the provision of the courses and training in communication, decision-making and leadership this requires. The experience I acquired in this work turned out to be essential. Nowadays, the main priority lies in the personal development of a person. We are living in a period in which the individual is going through a process of transformation, during which the well-known ways of living and working together disappear, making room for new ones.

During my studies, I was already aware that the processes that take place in and between people only illuminate one side of the question. There had to be another, more fundamental side I did not know about. The problem which confronted me became even more intriguing when, in one of my textbooks, I read that in counselling, the determining factor as to whether the client is able to connect to himself, thereby becoming able to take the necessary steps on the path of change and growth, is the relationship between the client and the counsellor — in particular the inherent attitude of the latter.

The truth of this was borne out by my own experience.

The question now was: what is it that occurs between people that, given certain circumstances, enables not only such a process of change to take place in the other but also gives him the strength to do it? It was soon clear to me that I would not find the answer in regular scientific thought. I had to move into an area of mental insights, of spirituality. But where to look? A long journey began.

Twenty-five to thirty years ago, there was hardly any literature in which personal development and the development of relationships and collaboration were linked to the spiritual element. Such books had yet to be written.

I began my search for answers in the East, in spiritual movements such as Hinduism, Buddhism and later Theosophy. But, although they opened my eyes to the reality of the spiritual world and enriched me personally, they did not provide the insights I was looking for. I found these only when I came across Rudolf Steiner's anthroposophy. I knew immediately that I could now connect what I saw in people and their mutual relationships to reality. I had found the framework through which my observations and experiences gained depth and meaning. And that was what I wanted.

But in this area, too, everything had yet to be worked out. I have been working on this for the past 25 years, as have many others. Very gradually, I was able to connect my experience of the development of the individual, relationships and collaboration to the spiritual element. Suddenly all the pieces of the puzzle fitted. This occurred in a flash of insight, such as the one I describe in the chapter on the reflection process.

What transpired? All development, be it in an individual, between people, in collaboration situations, in organizations or wherever, takes place according to fixed laws which point the way—a way in which something becomes visible and can be experienced. What is that something? It is the spirit which lives in everybody and everything, is recognized in all spiritual movements and can be summarized as 'the primeval source of all being'. Human development takes place so that this source can be active and reach expression in and between people, in organizations and in the greater whole of society and the world. Thence it elevates human life to higher realms of consciousness and existence.

I realized that everything we do or do not do, our entire life and work, alone and together, is subject to this process and constitutes the meaning of our life on earth.

I have planned this book so that the development, intrinsically describing the same process, becomes visible on three levels. Part One describes personal development in phases, differentiating between the path of the woman and that of the man. Part Two describes the laws behind the processes in relationships and teams and Part Three the phases in the development of organizations, both commercial and ideal-based.

I have tried to describe the processes in the various phases in such a way that everyone can recognize them in their own lives and in their collaboration with others. Through it all, the other reality becomes visible and tangible: the world of the spirit.

My experience as a trainer and organization-coach is that the laws I describe at three different levels can be a great help in recognizing and understanding the various processes. Gradually, as they become familiar, these can become the tools for a methodical approach and assistance in the necessary process of change we all have to go through in our time.

This book could not have been written without intensive interchange between a great many people. In the first place, I would like to thank the people I was able to work with in organizations in The Netherlands, Belgium, Scotland, Wales and England. I want to thank especially the Oaklands Park Community in Newnham-on-Severn for their support.

I must also thank Hans Schauder, Werner Cruijsberg, Leopold Koopman, Pauline Fock, Henny Hammen, Anneke van Gessel, Hans Stolp, Rob Bootsma and Jan Ritzema and, of course, him who is most dear to me.

They all stimulated me by their warm interest and involvement or helped me in practical ways to write this book.

Margarete van den Brink

The Seven Phases of Spiritual Development

1. Undivided unity
2. The old group
3. The 'I'-person
4. The transformation
5. The spiritual Self
6. The new community
7. Differentiated unity

Non nobis Domine, non nobis, sed nomini tuo da gloriam

(Not unto us, O Lord, not unto us, but unto Thy name give glory)

PART ONE: PERSONAL DEVELOPMENT

1. The Seven Phases of One's Personal Life-path

Phase 1: Undivided unity

As new-born infant you are entirely ensconced in an atmosphere of unity. This unity can be compared to a sort of heavenly state of security and warmth in which there is no differentiation between you and your surroundings. Unconscious of yourself, you feel at one with your mother and the rest of your surroundings, a state of total dependence. Very gradually, slight changes occur. The baby becomes a toddler, stands on its own feet and learns to walk and talk. It explores its surroundings, thereby manifesting its 'I'. This 'I' is the strength that will eventually turn it into an independent personality. The first experiments of a child towards personal independence are possible because there is a mother, father or other carer in the background. They see to it that the child comes to no harm and that it can return safely to the loving care of the parent(s) with whom it feels at one.

The ego

Around the second or third year, the child begins to say 'I'. This leads to its 'stubborn' phase. Not only does it show resistance, it is able to say 'no' and definitely *not* want to do something. This too is an important step towards independence. By saying 'no' and showing resistance, the child is in opposition to its environment for the first, and only short, time. A very brave deed! After all, for its own well-being and development it is entirely dependent on those parents or carers. By this deed of resistance, the child experiences for the first time something of a distance between itself and its surroundings, with which it had up till then been at one. Psychology has taught us how important it is for the further development of one's personality how parents and carers react to these first signs of independence. A child feels itself more or less at one with the surrounding world up to the age of six or seven. The process of becoming independent, however, is still going on.

Phase 2: The old group

Growing up, you are part of a group; in the first instance your family.

At school, too, you are part of a group: the school itself, your class, your own group of friends, the sports or other clubs of which you are a member. As a member of these sub-groups, you are placed in the dilemma I have just described. On the one hand, you are intensely connected to your family, school, class or group of friends, on the other you sometimes want to be alone and to do things alone — listening to music in your room, playing computer games, reading or going fishing early in the morning. Each child has different preferences. Some live for the feeling of belonging to their group, others are more loosely involved. Be that as it may, in this phase it is still very important for the development of the growing child that it is part of a group and knows it belongs and is accepted.

One characteristic of groups is that they have certain values, norms and rules to which members must adhere if they wish to be accepted. This also applies to school. For instance, you have to wear certain makes of clothes or shoes in order to belong to a particular group, or to employ specific language or mannerisms. In other words, you have to comply with the rules and norms of the group; otherwise you will not be accepted. Your position in the group makes for clarity and gives you a feeling of security. This is important, because the feeling of unity with the surrounding world is gradually falling apart. On the other hand, you can sometimes feel imprisoned in a group, hampered in your movements.

Self-esteem in relation to the surroundings
Meanwhile, your self-esteem and the picture you have of yourself are developing. In this phase, this picture and self-esteem are largely influenced by externals: your looks, your clothes and behaviour, but also your surroundings — what other people, such as your parents, teachers and the children of your group expect from you and reflect back to you.

In this phase, you start wondering who you are. At this age many children idolize film stars or television and sport heroes, sometimes even a particular teacher with whom they can identify and who they try to emulate.

Phase 2 is the phase in which you no longer feel entirely at one with everything around you, as you did in phase 1, but identify more with smaller units: your family or relatives and the other groups to which you belong, or with certain people who are special to you.

It is clear that for your self-esteem and feeling of well-being, you are entirely dependent on the grown-ups and children around you and the relationships you have with them.

Phase 3: The 'I'-person

At the start of puberty, around the age of 12 or 13, there is a new step towards personal independence, in spite of the fact that you are still very dependant on the people and children around you. At school you learnt to read, write and do arithmetic and to have your say in a discussion. Your intellectual capacities were roused, with the result that yet more distance was put between you and the surrounding world. You begin to form your own opinions and judgements and this means that you clash with the opinions of others, such as parents, teachers and perhaps other youngsters in your group. The struggle for increasing independence manifests itself in this period in the fact that you try to loosen the ties to the group with which you had up till now been most closely connected: your parents and your family. You oppose one or both of your parents. This process in phase 3 is similar to the 'stubborn' period in phase 1. This is only natural, since the developments in phase 3 are a continuation of the process of becoming independent that started in phase 1. By gradually separating yourself from your surroundings, placing yourself apart from the world and other people and standing your ground, you, as you grow up, develop your own personality, your self-esteem and thus your own identity.

Personal independence
Most young people leave home between their eighteenth and twentieth year. Full of dedication and enthusiasm, they immerse themselves in 'real' life, doing what they have set out to do. You start work or further education or a combination of the two. You have as yet little self-knowledge or experience of life, so the confrontation with the

world must teach you what can and cannot be done, who you are and what you are capable of. Experimenting and experiencing are the important facets of these first years of independence. The intensive interaction with other people and other situations makes you more conscious of yourself as an individual, increasingly able to build up a life of your own. During this period, there is once more a greater gap between you and your surroundings but your self-esteem is still extremely dependent on what other people think of you. In order to show who you are and what you can do, you want to score, competing with your colleagues or others and come off best. You also want others to recognize and value your achievements.

Ego

In the second half of your twenties, the tendency towards independence becomes stronger because your own thinking becomes more profound. You think about your experiences and the things you come across. You have a better overview. Your analytical capacity increases. You see things more objectively, weigh things up, take your own stand and make decisions. During this period, many people make fundamental decisions that are of great influence on the rest of their lives: the choice of a partner, whether or not to start a family, buy a house, plan a career, and so on. Thus in this phase you are intensely occupied with yourself and with planning your life. You are therefore very egocentric. Everything revolves around yourself and your presentation in, and in relationship to, the world. The 'I' that you have developed up to that point and which has become stronger during those years is therefore called the 'ego'. This concentration on your ego is shown by your continual efforts to prove yourself, the fact that you are

combative and convinced that you are right. You enjoy the
excitement of challenging others.

Status

Together with the developments in this phase, there is
often a susceptibility for outward appearances. You strive
for a certain position in your work, you buy a car and a
house to correspond to that status and you also choose the
sort of holidays that are expected of someone in your
position. All these externals show who you are, what you
can do and the position you have attained. With this, you
show the world, but also yourself, a certain picture of
yourself. In this phase, too, you are still fairly dependent on
your surroundings and what other people think of you.

In the course of your thirties, you have gained some
experience of life. You have learnt to know and use your
own strengths. You have some knowledge of the world,
what makes people tick and how they react. You think you
are in control of your life and yourself.

Then, very gradually, this situation changes.

Phase 4: The transformation

Uneasiness and inner questioning

This change starts with a vague feeling of uneasiness that
you do not understand. After all, from the outside everything appears to be fine. In the first instance, you suppress
these threatening feelings. Thoughts such as: Is this all? Is
this what I live for? What do I want from life? come to the
surface. These too are suppressed. You work a little harder,
have an extra drink or watch the telly till late at night.
Sometimes the negation of these feelings can last a long

time. Some people even manage to do this up to far in their fifties. In spite of the flight from yourself, however, the inner unrest returns with some regularity. The reason for this is that, deep inside you, there is a struggle between your ego and a completely different aspect of yourself. This inner struggle manifests itself in many different ways. Firstly, as insecurity and fear. For instance, you feel that everything is still all right but that it can be over at any moment. You think: Am I still up to it? Or you suddenly realize that you are already over 40 and 'it' still has not happened. You do not really know what 'it' is. You want something but what in the world is it? Where do you look? Or you realize: there must be something else, but what and where?

During this period, many people are confronted with a feeling of emptiness and weakness, a feeling that they have lost control of life and therefore also the meaning of their own life. Looking for answers to all these questions takes a long time, usually years. You feel the need for a reorientation of yourself and your life. You want to assess not only your past, but also your present position and what you want from the future.

You explore: What sort of life have I led up to now? What was right and where did I miss the boat? What are my strengths and weaknesses? What are my qualities? As far as the present is concerned, you may ask: What sort of person do I want to be? What are the values and principles which are important to me? Where do we come from, where are we going? To what do I want my life to contribute? And for the future: If I want to achieve or change this or that, which characteristics or capabilities will I need? What do I need to develop? How and where could I put these new ideas and values into practice? What needs to be done?

All the restlessness and insecurity caused by these

questions and impulses turn your existence and all you have achieved till then upside down. For many people this results in a crisis. They feel that they have come to an internal standstill, unable to go any further and in need of therapy. This crisis is necessary in order to facilitate the next steps in your development as a person.

The real Self

Where do all these new questions and impulses come from? I have already mentioned that they stem from an inner conflict between your ordinary self, your ego, and quite another aspect living in the depths of your soul. This other aspect is your spiritual Self, also called your 'higher self'. Your spiritual Self is your deepest being. It is that part of you which makes you a unique individual, that which you really are. You could also call it the ultimate aim of your life. Carl Gustav Jung said, 'Self is also the aim of life, since it is the complete expression of the destiny one calls the individual.'[1]

This spiritual Self is characterized by qualities such as consciousness, strength, energy, truth, honesty, justice, beauty, freedom, commitment, goodness, loving. Since it is part of the divine-spiritual world, it is an active, moral, creative power of consciousness that lives in the depths of our soul and of which we are largely unaware. It gives meaning to our lives and empowers inner development, consciousness and strength. In our times, this very real aspect demands recognition and appreciation. It wants to become active within us so that we may become what we really are. Questions such as: 'Who am I?' and 'What do I want from life?' can be recognized as impulses with which this spiritual Self shakes us awake and shows us that the most important part has yet to be realized. After all, we have not yet reached our goal in life.

The deeper and more intense your dealings with the real questions are, the more this spiritual Self, this power of spiritual consciousness in your innermost soul, will increase and come to life.

From outside to inside
This development work on yourself, this spiritual activity, at the same time marks an inner process of transformation. In the course of time, the powers of the self-seeking ego wane and slowly but surely the powers of your spiritual Self are freed in you. A well has sprung in your innermost being and begins to flow. Gradually you feel freer, richer, stronger and sometimes even happier. Your life starts to have more meaning. This turning-point or transformation also alters the point of reference in your life. Up till then, your self-esteem and identity were largely dependent on your surroundings, your status and a great many material things, whereas now you are less dependent on them and they gradually lose their central place. This shows that your point of reference is being shifted from the outside to the inside by this process, from your surroundings to your own inner world. The support and anchorage you used to look for in the outside world you can now increasingly find in your own soul, your own inner world. To your surprise, this gives you a new sort of feeling of balance and security. As you learn to trust it, you increasingly start to live from this new inner strength.

Phase 5: The spiritual Self

As you constantly reflect on all sorts of important issues and work on yourself, your real Self grows in you. One of the results of this is that your inner life and that in the outside world become more and more connected. This was not so in phase 4. There, there were two separate worlds and this caused inner strife. How can I be more myself in my post as manager? How can I combine my need to be alone with living with my partner? And more, similar questions.

Distancing oneself

Another important element of this continual reflection is that you become increasingly objective about yourself and the things around you. You learn to distinguish between what is really important and what is not. This means that you can steer your life and your relationships with others more consciously. And again you experience this waxing power as an inner awakening which provides new strengths. Ben Verbong, director of the Passion Plays in Tegelen (Netherlands) recalls this process: 'I awoke when I discovered that I could stand above things, not only in them. When I began to direct plays, I also got the feeling that I could largely direct my own life. The feeling that you can gain control, that you can steer things to a great extent and not just be steered.'[2]

Inner balance

Another characteristic of your spiritual growth is that your inner world becomes increasingly balanced. This does not mean that there is no longer a struggle. You have now come to know a large part of your own drawbacks and weaknesses and no longer hide them. But learning to deal with them in the right way demands daily practice and patience. New problems are always arising which demand attention. And once again it is reflection which leads you on: What is this all about? What do I feel about it? What do I want to do about it, what not? What is important? How can I best deal with the other person? Amongst other things, this balance is evident in the way these and other questions are met and dealt with in a quieter and more sensible way. Inner peace also comes from not being so susceptible to the feverishness and delusion of everyday life and from the fact that there is no need for you to prove yourself. You like to be alone now and then, to think, get ideas, develop a vision, formulate ideals. You listen more and more to the inner voice which comes from your spiritual Self. In this phase, many people become interested in spirituality or religion and try to learn more about them.

Values and principles

The questions you continually ask yourself show that you turn inwards for a particular search. You always seem to be looking for something which can give you clarification and guidance: a sort of inner compass for your journey. What is this inner compass? It is formed by the values and principles that are important to you. Thus the values behind the questions mentioned above could be: truth, honesty, doing the right thing, helping someone who is struggling, and so on. At this stage of your life, values and qualities as a motive for doing or not doing things become more and more important. They inspire and guide you.

I once asked a policeman who was involved daily with serious road accidents, 'What is your motive for continuing with this difficult work?' After a moment's thought, he said, 'To determine what really happened and see justice done, both towards the victim and the perpetrator.' Truth and justice: values and principles which guide him and his working life. Qualities of his higher Ego, expressed and experienced through his ordinary personality.

Personal leadership

Becoming spiritually active through reflection thus leads to your being able to step back and rise above your own ego, able to understand more. You become more balanced and restful in yourself, you can steer yourself and your life on the basis of values and principles. This is personal leadership. You show yourself increasingly capable of mastering your own soul, your innermost being. The powers generated by this are expressed in wisdom and commitment to others.

Wisdom

Through your spiritual growth, you can fathom and survey more. You are focused on the future and perspectives. You are conscious of your mission and have an aim that transcends yourself. Your vision inspires others and sets them to work. Your words often have great meaning. With your belief in values, ideals and qualities, you also awaken these in others. You are like an Olympic flame from which others can light their torches. In other words, you are an example of the working of wisdom in man and what it can achieve.[3]

Phase 6: The new community

Commitment to others

People who have developed something important in themselves and thereby found themselves, are free to help others. At this stage of your development, you can put yourself aside when necessary and help others by stimulating their development, which becomes as important to you as your own. Since you have learnt to know and accept yourself, you can do the same towards others.

You can see the other as he is, with all his good, weak, strong and as yet unknown qualities, accept them and let them stand. Strangely enough, if the other is allowed to be himself, sooner or later he will feel impelled to acknowledge his less developed qualities and set to work on them — not because you pointed them out, but because the honest impression you formed of him awakens the impulse for development. Characteristic of your way of dealing with people is that you are more likely to ask questions than to state your view and, in the case of problems, you are ready to sympathize and think along with them, rather than come up with solutions. You are not dominant or moulding but show a willingness to help. Scoring is no longer important. Thankfully, you have left that behind.

Phase 7: Differentiated unity

Awareness and care for the greater whole
The more the strength of awareness of your higher Self awakens in you, the larger the areas it can encompass. You realize what life and the world is about. You see that every person, and his mission in life, is an important link in the life of humanity as a whole. You know that where it is all going also depends on you. You want to play an active part. You are always thinking: What is now essential? What is at stake? What can I contribute? The choices you make are usually linked to what you see as the deeper meaning of your life, your mission in life. You could thus

leave for South America to put your knowledge and experience in ecological agriculture at their disposal there, or you could innovate sustainable policy in your company, start a meditation centre for working and personal development, or some such thing.

2. Stephan Peijnenburg's Steps

The steps described in the last chapter can be found in almost everyone's life. Sometimes not all of them, but certainly a number of them. As an example, this is the story of Stephan Peijnenburg. In April 2000, as the last Peijnenburg of the family business, Koninklijke Peijnenburg's Koekfabriek (a well-known make of Dutch honey-cake), and 42 years old, he left for another job. Six months later, the rest of the family — consisting of his father, four brothers and a sister — decided to sever all ties with the 117-year-old business and sell their shares. Stephan admits it was an enormous step: 'But the Peijnenburgs go all the way or not at all. That means that you commit yourself for one hundred per cent to the business or you disappear.'

Is this all?

For 17 years he enjoyed working in the factory in Geldrop, until he suddenly asked himself: Is this all? Do I want to spend another 15 years making and selling honey-cake? Or is there more to life? Peijnenburg: 'Then I said I wanted to take a sabbatical for half a year. If you go on working, you don't get the opportunity for reflection. I have four small children and I imagined what it would be like when they were my age. Things happen so fast and not really in a direction I approve of. Through drastic individualization, society is beginning to become egotistical. This is not the most sensible way and I was looking for something to get people to think about it. In any case, I wanted to contribute.

My children? Yes, I want to set them a good example. That is also a reason.'

Many discussions with father, brothers and sister, all passive shareholders in the firm, follow. His siblings, in particular, understand and support his wish for something more profound. A good temporary director is available and the firm's prospects are good. At a delicious family dinner, the decision is toasted.

The choice for a personal mission

After three months, Peijnenburg is sure he does not want to go back. He has looked around and found the idealistic Max Havelaar Foundation (a Fair Trade organization). He says he had not decided beforehand to leave the family business. But once the decision to do something completely different had been made, all sorts of things happened. 'Things come to you by themselves. The resistance you felt before melts away.'

Half a year after asking himself those crucial questions, Peijnenburg is Director of Marketing and Communication, and two years later General Director with Max Havelaar. He brought with him the experience and expertise he had from the food trade. 'I very much wanted to use these in my new job. This did not necessarily have to be a top position, so long as I was able to add something to the existing knowledge and experience.'

That which is possible at Max Havelaar's—selling food at prices which show respect for the producer, the small farmer—is, according to Peijnenburg, impossible in a commercial context.

The traditional food market is extremely competitive. It

is practically impossible for ideals to be implemented. Not even in Peijnenburg's Koekfabriek. His job with Max Havelaar is especially attractive to Stephan because it is anomalous to the business world. Peijnenburg: 'I want to be able to appeal to managers' social responsibility, for giving their employees a decent living, for their surroundings. That sort of thing. I see consumers and producers very slowly but increasingly becoming aware of this. Max Havelaar is playing a part to which I can contribute.'[4]

What different phases can be seen here?

In the first place, Stephan Peijnenburg's story shows a person taking the step of moving away from the family tradition (phase 2). Working for 17 years in his own family business demonstrates that the family ties were very strong. So does his remark: 'We Peijnenburgs go all the way or not at all. Either you commit yourself one hundred per cent or you disappear.' It shows that he strongly identifies with the characteristics of his family group (phase 2). However, at a certain point he goes his own individual way (phase 3), as his brothers and sister did before him. He reflects on what is essential to him in life and how he wishes to contribute with his experience and capacities. By means of these reflections, he passes through the process of transformation (phase 4) and discovers the principles and values that are really important to him. His own personal vision and mission become clear and he brings them into practice (phase 5). With his ideals, such as care for a decent livelihood for his employees, care for their surroundings and so on, he touches on the ideals of phase

6. But above all, he wants to awaken people, consumers, managers and food producers, give them something to think about and, like him, realize that they have a responsibility for the development of society. That brings him finally to phase 7: his awareness and care, as an individual, for the well-being of the larger whole of which he is a part.

3. Laws of Development

Our life as a human being, an individual, runs its course in certain phases. This is not a haphazard process but follows patterns in which one phase connects to another and the next phase emerges from the previous one. This is shown schematically on page 36.

The essentials of the laws which govern each phase are, in general terms, as follows.

Phase 1 is the situation all of us have passed through: the sensation of unity with everything and everybody around us. You cannot say you *feel* at one with your surroundings because you are not yet conscious of yourself. The situation is clearest in the state before birth, when you lived in complete unawareness in your mother's body, and for a short time after birth.

Therefore this phase is called *undivided unity*.

Phase 2 shows that, as a person, we are part of various groups during our lifetime. Characteristic of living in groups in phase 2 is that you largely feel at one with the other members of the group and strongly identify with them and the current values, norms, ideas and rules. You think, feel and act to a great extent as the others do. You are hardly conscious of yourself as a separate being, an individual. You may say 'I' but you really mean 'we'. People who still live strongly in phase 2 often speak in the 'we' idiom, even when this is out of place and 'I' would be more appropriate.

This shows that you find it difficult to distinguish between yourself and the group and that awareness of the male and the female in us, to the full. But as her life unfolds, a woman's female characteristics come to the fore in the first instance, while the male characteristics remain somewhat in the background. The same applies to the man. He too first develops his male characteristics, while the greater part of the female ones remain in the background. This does not mean that that there are no (young) women with obvious male characteristics or (young) men with female qualities. One's constitution often plays an important role as well and in practice there is usually some sort of mix.

In general, one could say that as men and women develop personally in the course of their lives and become aware of the hidden characteristics of the opposite sex, they will develop them and integrate them into their personality. Then men become not only rational but also sensitive. Women will no longer be dependent on other people's opinions but become decisive and self-aware.

The above sketch of the differences between men and women and their background is necessary for understanding why they go through the seven phases in a different way. So as not to repeat myself too often, I emphasize those phases in which the differences are most marked: phases 2 to 4.

But first some general remarks on phase 1. As a baby, every man and woman goes through the phase of undivided unity. It is interesting to note that scientific research shows that differentiation between male and female only appears in the third prenatal month of the embryo.[15] Before then, the embryo is sexless. That means that until then the male and female principle are an undivided unity in the nascent human being!

The seven phases

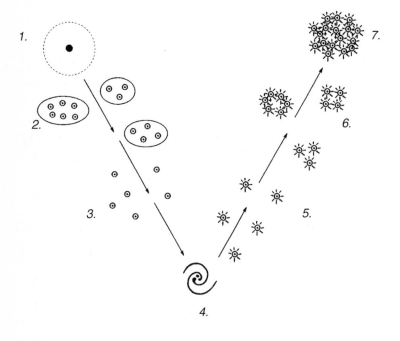

your self is still weak. It is also true that you are not seen by others as an individual—a person in your own right, another. Opinions that differ from those of the group are not tolerated. Group situations such as this can be found everywhere: in families and households, in religious and other groups and communities, idealistic or otherwise, in societies and clubs, but also in teams within a company or business.

This phase is called *the old group* because the individual is still subservient to the group.

Phase 3 shows that sooner or later we gradually detach ourselves from this sort of group and come to stand on our own as an individual. The characteristic element in phase 3 is that you place yourself in *opposition* to others. Now you want to distinguish between yourself and the other in order to get to know and express your own self. You do this by firmly stating your opinions and standpoints, discussing viewpoints and proving yourself in various ways. It is the phase in which you develop your ego, your everyday personality. This phase is therefore also called *the ego*, indispensable for the development of the next steps.

Phase 4 is the turning-point. An old part of you grinds to a halt and comes to an end and a new element in you wants to be born. The two intertwined signs in the diagram on page 36 symbolize this. The past that has made you the person you now are wants to be recognized and absorbed. As for the future, the strengths of your real, spiritual Self—the dot . in the middle—want to be developed by means of impulses living within and new powers. The turning-point is accompanied by a feeling of crisis. Your foothold is shaky, you may experience problems with your health or in relationships, or stress, but at the same time you open up inside. Initially you do not know how to deal with all this chaos and change, nor do you know where it will all lead. Phase 4 is called *the transformation*.

Phase 5 develops as the process of reflection and working on yourself increasingly causes the stronger self-awareness and wisdom of your higher Self to come to life. You also become less egocentric. Since you have found yourself, you can relinquish your ordinary self, your ego, and rise above it. As the powers of your higher Self increase, you emanate something which can help others. The diagram shows that in this phase you begin to 'shine'. You change from being a taker to being a giver.

Phase 5 is that of the development of *the spiritual Self*.

Phase 6 emerges from phase 5. The more you find yourself and live by the higher powers in you, the more interest you take in others. No longer are *you* the most important, but the other and his struggle, for whom you can be of service, thanks to the powers you have developed. Not only is there greater awareness, and therefore light, in this phase, but you can now really give love to other people. Rollo May once described love in the following way: 'Love is the joy that the other is there and the inner willingness to see his worth and development as being just as important as your own.'[5] That is what you develop in this phase. People who develop their awareness and light powers in phase 5 and the loving powers of phase 6 obviously treat each other in a completely different way from what they did in earlier stages. If they form groups together, these are completely different to the groups in phase 2. The characteristic in phase 6 is that not the group but the individual takes centre stage. A phase 6 group is first and foremost a collection of independent individuals in whom the powers of the

spiritual Self-awareness, honesty, wisdom and so on—
have fully developed, as well as the capacity for a liberat-
ing, acknowledging and supportive love for others and
each other. It is clear that these new relationships will lead
to an entirely different way of living and working together
and that a new sort of community will emerge. I use the
word 'will', since we are talking of developments which
can be envisaged, which are in fact already under way, but
which will only be fully realized in the future, as our own
development progresses. This will become clearer in the
course of this book and through examples.

Because of the new type of social relationships and a new
feeling of solidarity between the individual members,
phase 6 is called *the new community.*

Phase 7 again emerges from the previous one. We can as
yet only imagine it, although, as the examples show, we are
already working on it. The more people find each other as
individuals in groups or communities in this new way, the
bigger such entities will become. It will be a situation in
which the spiritual powers—awareness, clarity, freedom—
and moral values such as honesty, integrity, justice, etc.
but, above all, truly unselfish love will prevail.

Because of this, people will feel united, but united in
diversity, since each individual will express the spirit in his
or her own unique way. And as the spirit—although different in each individual—is one in all, they will feel as one.
As a self-aware, *differentiated unity.*

4. Broad Outlines

The seven phases, reduced to essentials, show that our road in life is not one of chance but one of development with a special meaning. It begins at a certain point and takes us further on our way inwards. A few broad outlines will make this clearer.

From dependence via independence to mutual involvement

You begin life as a human being in total dependence on others. If there is no one to love you and look after you, you cannot survive.

You grow up. With the development of your own 'I' — first in its lower stage as ego, later in the higher as spirit Self — your dependence on your surroundings and on other people gradually diminishes. As you reach phase 3, the ego-phase, your independence grows. You stand on your own feet and can manage without others. At least, you think you can.

Usually you revise this feeling in phase 4. You land in a personal or relationship crisis, and to your surprise you seek contact and communication with people who understand you and your situation. These people also want real contact with you. Suddenly, you realize how much people need each other for this mutual process and how dependent we are on each other in order to be able to take the next steps. This applies not only to your personal life but also to your work. 'Being dependent on others' now has a different content. Your greatest fear is still that you revert to a former phase of dependence and thus be the victim of the power of others over you. But if you can retain your independence and remain a free spirit, that changes. The new powers of your spiritual Self ground you in phase 4 and, from there, more firmly in yourself. They make it possible for you to feel independent and free but at the same time to acknowledge and accept that you need the other for your development and to be able to do that which you wish to attain. And this applies equally to the other. Stephen Covey describes the road of dependence, independence and interdependence and commitment very well in his book *The Seven Habits of Highly Effective People.*[6]

From outward to inward and outward again

Phases 1 to halfway through phase 4 are aimed at developing your ordinary 'I' — your personality, your everyday ego. The movement is from the outside inward. You take, as it were, that from your surroundings which you need for your personal development. Phases 1, 2 and 3 and part of 4 could be called the ego-period, in which you 'take' from others. In phase 4 there is a reversal. Inwardly, you 'grasp' the powers of your spiritual Self and start to develop them. The 'spirit' is alive *in* you and *for* you. But not only that! It lives in you and wants to work through you for the well-being of others and for the well-being of larger entities, such as society, the world, the earth.[7] In phase 4, therefore, you turn from the inside outward and again inward in order to fulfil your mission in life and to put your qualities and capacities at the disposal of others and the greater good. In this way, from being an ego-person, a 'taker', you gradually become a 'giver', one in whom the spirit is at work.

From unawareness via self-awareness to inclusive spiritual awareness

Obviously the seven phases are also the road to the development of awareness.

In phase 1 you are entirely unaware, also unaware of yourself. Then you develop awareness of the group: 'we think that' (phase 2). Self-awareness follows: 'I want, I think that' (phase 3). Your awareness is still almost entirely focused on yourself and that which pertains to your life. Through the transformation in phase 4 and the spiritual enrichment this brings about, you develop an increasingly inclusive spiritual awareness in phases 5, 6 and 7. This increased awareness makes you more committed to your surroundings. You feel more and more responsible for the well-being of others. This can be seen in Stephan Peijnenburg's steps. All this leads to your being able to commit yourself to an increasing number of people, groups and larger entities and contribute to their development.

More than one step at a time

The fact that life is so complicated nowadays is borne out by the fact that different parts of us are living in different phases. Looking back on your own development, you will see that you do not go through each step one by one, like, for instance, the classes at school.

In practice, it turns out that in a particular period a

certain phase is predominant, but that you are at the same time also living in previous ones. For instance, you sometimes act or feel as if you were in phase 2. Reflection on your past in phase 4 makes you aware of how dependent you still are on others, authorities or people important to you; in other words, you are still partly living in phase 2. At the same time, you might notice how difficult it is for you to deal with authoritarian people and how reactive you are in your contacts with them. You revert to certain limiting reaction patterns. The knowledge that you do this can be very confronting and shocking but it does not denigrate you as a person. It only shows that you are on the way, developing. You are becoming the one you really are. To summarize, you could say that during certain periods of your life one particular phase is predominant but that, as you reflect and work on yourself, you regularly revert to undeveloped sides in yourself that are still in earlier phases. Our human development is clearly not a linear but a cyclic process. Your as yet undeveloped sides are 'brushed up' as you become aware of them and pay attention to them.

By letting light—in other words, spiritual awareness— fall on them and practising different behaviour, you let this spiritual part of you grow. Then, for instance, you learn to face an authoritarian person in a pro-active instead of a reactive way and adopt a different inner attitude.

Carl Jung calls this working on oneself the individualization process. By this he means that we humans become 'whole' by working hard on ourselves; we become an undivided unit on its own, an individual. This process of invidualization occurs when, by means of active reflection about yourself and what you come across in life, you manage to integrate all the loose, aware and unaware parts

of your personality. The wholeness achieved by this process of integration creates in you this higher, undivided
unity: your Individuality, your real spiritual Self, that
which you really are.[8]

Getting stuck

There are, of course, people who, in spite of all kinds of
signals, do not have the courage to look at themselves, to
change and grow. There are women who are afraid of
losing their femininity if they develop their ego. They
prefer to remain in phase 2, dependent on others, rather
than learn to think for themselves and make their own
decisions.

Another example is men in their forties who hold on
desperately to the values and attitudes belonging to phase
3, the ego-phase. With ever-renewed strength, they try to
show what they can do, to demonstrate that they are not
yet past it. This often succeeds for a while but after their
thirties their behaviour becomes increasingly forced,
making further growth more difficult or even impossible.
Eventually, this flight takes its toll and all sorts of psy-
chosomatic ailments surface, such as heart and vascular
disease, gastric and intestinal complaints, backache and so
on or psychic problems such as frustration, cynicism and
tyranny. Since they have not found the meaning of their
own lives, they have lost faith in themselves and the world
and show this all the time.[9]

Fear of regression

You will understand more of people's behaviour as you
realize that everyone is afraid of regressing entirely to an

earlier stage of development, thus losing their new powers of awareness and ego.

Hans Knibbe, a *gestalt* therapist, says he often asks the following question of training-groups: 'Imagine that all of us here are part of one organism. We cannot become separated from each other, just as my hand cannot be separated from my arm. What does this feel like? How do you react to this?'

Invariably, he says, the majority are horrified. They often feel they are no longer free, that they must give up their individuality and that the whole situation is far too intimate. Often it transpires that there is a deep — and up till then unconscious — hate towards the others.[10] Here again is this fear of regression to a much earlier phase, in this case maybe even phase 1. But why this horror and hate? This is also dictated by fear, fear not only of regression but of thereby reverting to the grip of older, even more unconscious powers at work in relationships between people — powers that try to prevent people from developing their own 'I' and independent spirit.

That such powers are very real is, for example, undisguisedly manifest in the way the Taliban government in Afghanistan treated the women in that country. They excluded them from everything: the street, public life, society, work and education, provided no care for them and swathed them in garments which made them completely invisible, both inside and out. This was a conscious measure to wipe out everything these women had so far developed, in particular their own personality, their ego. In this way, they were intended to revert spiritually to much older, earlier phases of development. Needless to say, this caused these women immense psychic and spiritual suffering.

When development is halted, repressed, deep fear is bred—fear of losing oneself. Such fear engenders hate, deep hate for those who cause this suffering.

Negative, adverse forces

Some people who look at the diagram of the seven phases think: once I have passed through the transformation stage, phase 4, that's it. The rays in the diagram show that then the sun shines permanently and life becomes much more agreeable. However, reality is different. Every development towards a higher and positive goal also has its lower, negative sides or forces. This was already obvious from the section on getting stuck in a certain phase. When there is no progression, regression sets in. There is no middle way. People who get stuck in phase 3 experience increasing health problems and negative moods. The same is true of people whose development is held back by their environment. The impotent anger and the resultant hate become stifling and engender a great deal of negative energy which seeks a way out.

The reality of negative, adverse forces can also be seen in the increasing violence of young people. You can prove yourself in phase 3 by presenting yourself positively to the world. You can, however, also do this in a negative way. Violence is also a way of showing the world your power. The harder the violence, the stronger your own self-esteem. A 23-year-old man who committed senseless violence said, 'Why should I pity someone I beat up? I say to myself: if he were in my place, he wouldn't care about me either. I want power; that is a great feeling.'[11]

Together with the growth of positive spiritual powers—

the light of awareness, honesty, loving commitment—the dark, aggressive and destructive powers also grow in us. Therefore the road in phases 5, 6 and 7 does not become easier, but more difficult. Someone once said: the road to the source is upstream. You can only develop honesty if you have also known dishonesty. Love only if you have experienced and overcome lack of love and evil. Thus the road, even after step 4, is one against resistance, demanding a great deal of trouble and effort. Chögyam Trungpa said of this road: 'Do not think the journey is short. One must have the heart of a lion to follow this unusual road, for it is very long ... One plods on with difficulty in a state of awe, sometimes laughing, sometimes crying.'[12]

5. Men and Women Pass Through the Seven Phases in Different Ways

In general, men and women are different and also go through the seven phases in their lives differently. Before going further into this, I will give you examples to show what their intrinsic differences are. One shows how a woman enters a room where she has never been and how a man does that. The second shows the different ways in which they buy shoes.

Coming into a room

A woman enters a room. She takes a quick look at it and registers the scene. She sees the furniture, the colour of the upholstery, what is on the walls, what sort of people there are. At the same time, she senses the atmosphere and decides whether she likes it or not. Not until she has this subjective picture does she look for a place to sit down. A man enters a room. He chooses a seat and goes to it. Then he looks round. He focuses on something, studies it and goes on to something else. Thus he gradually builds up a picture of the room. His feelings about it do not usually come into it.

Buying shoes

A man decides he needs new shoes. He decides beforehand exactly what he wants: they must not cost more than a certain amount, must not be made of suede, must have broad soles and must be comfortable. He goes to a shop and tells the salesman what he wants. He then makes his choice from the selection offered and leaves.

A woman who wants new shoes goes to town. She has some idea what she is looking for but does not yet know exactly. She must find out by looking at a large number of shoes. She goes to different shops, and after four, five or more decides to go back to the second and buy the pair she liked most for various reasons. She goes home and shows the shoes to her partner. If he does not like them or she changes her own mind, she returns to the shop and exchanges them for another pair.

The first example shows that a man's position in the world is quite different to that of a woman. She first registers and undergoes the whole. Only then does she look at the constituent parts (for instance, where she wants to sit). From there, she places everything in relationship to the whole.

The man begins by registering the separate parts of the whole. He immediately goes to where he wants to sit and from there observes the various parts. By connecting the one to the other, he eventually forms a picture of the whole.

The example of buying shoes shows that a man thinks first before doing and makes decisions on the basis of criteria he has set himself. It is quite different for a woman. Before going to town, she is not clear what sort of shoes she actually wants. Usually she has no real criteria. The variety of choice must help make up her mind and her feelings play an important role.

An essential difference in both examples is that the important element for the woman is herself. Her feelings and her relationship to the whole or the number determine her choice and thus her relationship to the world. A man's personal feelings seem to have little or no influence. They often seem to remain outside his decision-making process and outside his relationship to the world.

Centrifugal and centripetal forces

So the psyches of men and women are completely different, actually opposed to each other. Why is this? According to many scientists, the differences are culturally determined. Boys and girls are from an early age conditioned to a male or female role and that determines the psyche.

Dr John Gray, relationship therapist and author of bestsellers on men, women and relationships, does not agree at all with this theory. Of course cultural influences play a part in development, he says, but they are not the cause of primary differences between men and women. If you really wish to understand these, you must realize that a centrifugal force is predominant in a woman's soul and a centripetal one in a man's.[13] I entirely agree with him. Centrifugal force moves from the centre outwards to the surroundings. In a woman, this means that by nature she moves away from herself and seeks connection to the people around her and the greater whole. Through this, she easily loses sight of herself. In contrast, the man, through the centripetal force, tends to turn inwards and thus away from the greater whole, the surroundings and other people. This centripetal force holds him together, to himself, and with the help of his will-power concentrates his thinking awareness. Thus he does not easily lose himself.

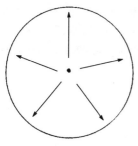

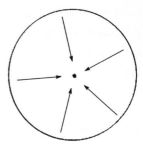

Woman's psyche　　　　　　　　　*Man's psyche*

Wolfgang Gädeke, author of the book *Sexuality, Partnership and Marriage*, agrees with John Gray's views on the male and female soul. The emphasis, he says, is on a woman's unity of soul and life forces.[14] By 'soul' he means what can be experienced through emotions, feelings, needs, aims, pleasure and displeasure, etc. It is that part of us that is very personal and that determines our relationship to something. The soul always has something to do with relationships. It is always in relation to something. One could say that the soul *is* relationship. The workings of the centrifugal force can also be found in this description of the woman's focus on relationships. Her focus on her surroundings also always includes their relationship to herself and her own feelings. How she feels about herself always plays a part in her contacts with other people or situations. By contrast, a man's natural focus is in the first place on the polarity of his 'I' and his physical body and not so much on his soul. His spiritual life, therefore, seems simpler. In the first instance, it is less differentiated, less structured, less fully formed and less colourful than that of a woman. Since he is more concerned with his physical body than with his soul, a man easily shuts himself off from his surroundings. This is strengthened by the centripetal forces in him. These concentrate and direct his will and his thinking awareness and converts his 'I'-force into being an independent person. Together, all these factors join in making the tendency towards individualization—the force that makes a human being into an 'I'-person—generally stronger in the man than in the woman.

Male and female characteristics

Connecting, receptive, warm, vulnerable, sensitive, emotional, intuitive, associative, involved with her surroundings, self-effacing, focused on relationships, on the other, on collaboration, on a process, communicative, open, malleable, what we call the female characteristics have all developed through the centrifugal working of the woman's soul.

Through the centripetal forces in a man, male characteristics such as analytical, logical thinking (taking things to pieces and putting them together again), reserved, intellectual, cool, pugnacious, competitive, assertive, efficient, aiming at goals and results, decisive, focused on himself and his business, power, and so on, develop.

Many men and women may say, however, even indignantly, that they do not recognize themselves in these one-sided male or female characteristics. Women feel they are not only emotional, but also intellectual. Men think they are not only analytical, but also sensitive. Many more examples can be given. Of course this is true. Every woman has characteristics we call male and every man those we call female. Potentially, we are able to develop both sides,

The man's road through the seven phases

Phase 2: The old group
In this phase, the boy is fully part of groups that have an important influence on him. The tendency towards individualization, however, which is so characteristic of male development, can already be seen. As a boy, you are encouraged to develop male characteristics—not to cry if you fall, to fight with other boys to show you can stand up to them, and so on. Your physical limits are put to the test in sports or dangerous adventures. But you can also spend hours alone, reading or listening to music.

Phase 3: The 'I'-person
In puberty the boy becomes increasingly conscious of himself as a 'man'. Your male characteristics come more strongly to the fore. The process of freeing yourself from the sheltered atmosphere of the family, especially from your mother, continues. It is not easy but it succeeds, because, as your male body develops and gets stronger, so do the centripetal forces. Thanks to your thinking and your will-power, you are increasingly able to analyse things in a businesslike way, to weigh them up, make choices and decide on your standpoint. This makes you more independent in yourself and less dependent on your surroundings. Phase 3, the phase in which you develop your ego, is the one in which you, as a man, feel yourself strongest.

The centripetal, focused force makes you forget everything around you except what you are aiming at. You therefore see the world, as John Gray puts it, through a tunnel.[16] Your concentrated consciousness only aims at one goal at a time. It could be compared to a thin laser-beam which illuminates only a fraction of something. You can only cope with one thing or problem at a time. If you concentrate on your work, you cannot at the same time pay attention to your surroundings, your partner, your children or to your relationship with them. If you want to pay attention to them, you have to make a conscious choice. If you do not, you remain shut away in yourself, solely occupied with your own affairs. A well-known example of this is the man who comes home from work, grabs the newspaper and disappears behind it. The concentration this gives him helps him deal with the day's events. This means, however, that he shuts himself up in his own world, which is often not appreciated by his family. Your capacity for concentration can make you determined, purposeful and efficient as a man, but also often blind to the needs of others and for priorities which are not immediately connected with the goal you think important. It makes you not only egocentric but also egoistic. Shutting yourself off from your surroundings also has another effect. It prevents you from noticing the signs of increasing unhappiness in your surroundings. Sometimes you only wake up when it is too late.

In the same way in which a man shuts himself off from his surroundings, he can also shut himself off from his own body and soul. You do not admit physical strain, emotions and pain, signals that something is wrong, but suppress them—as you do the ever-recurring feelings of unease and insecurity.

Phase 4: The transformation

In such a situation, the crisis accompanying the process of transformation in phase 4 usually comes as a great shock. All of a sudden something may happen. You may have a blackout or burn-out, become overworked, lose control in a drunken brawl, collapse as the result of an accident, or have problems in a relationship or at work. A great many emotions come to the surface. Some men wake up crying one day, suddenly realizing that the world has changed. Something inside you has broken through your ego-harness, causing a fall into your soul. You suddenly come to a place inside yourself where you have never been before and this causes fear and anxiety. You do not have the capacities to deal with all the forces living there and you do not know the way out. What has happened? The diagram below makes that clear. It shows and describes the various layers of the human soul.

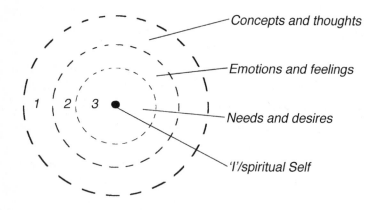

The outer ring (1) denotes concepts and thoughts. It is the part we are most conscious of. The layer below (2) is that of emotions and feeling. This layer is far less conscious than that of waking thoughts. Under that (3) is the even less conscious layer of the impulses, desires, needs and motives that steer your actions. In reality, of course, these areas are not separated like this. They work in and through each other and influence each other. The dot in the middle is the 'I', which contains the ordinary, everyday ego and the spiritual Self.

The diagram shows that up to the crisis you lived mostly in the outer ring, that of conscious thought, and that the needs and motives from the third layer were mostly aimed at your own activities or your work in the outside world. What happens in the crisis is that you 'fall through the floor', as it were, and suddenly land in the layer of emotions and feelings — soul forces which live in you too. From there, you come to layer 3 and the needs that belong to those emotions and feelings. Layer 2 is the real centre of the soul. It has already been described as the part which lets us humans form relationships, both with yourself as a person and with the people around you, the world and greater entireties.

In other words, 'the fall into your soul' brings you to an area where forces such as emotions and feelings live that enable you to feel and live with yourself and other people. You are thus able to step out of the one-sidedness which was characteristic of your development up till then. But you must consciously want to develop those facets in you. If you do, then characteristics will emerge such as making connections, giving warmth, being receptive, showing emotions and feelings, ability to form relationships, being open, communicative, intuitive and so on. 'Female' characteristics, in fact, which make completely new relationships with other people possible and enrich you.

In this phase, many men feel the need to have contact with someone else in order to come to grips with themselves through the other. They seek help or therapy or take part in groups, thus to get to know and deal with this 'female' part of themselves and to integrate it into their own personality. There is a lot to do in this phase, especially as the existential questions mentioned in the previous chapters need to be looked at. These questions come from the core, the spiritual Self.

Why is it important that a man goes through this dramatic stage? Because it is the only way to find your real Self. If you remain stuck in your outward, abstract thinking patterns, you will not succeed. You will then be too shut off and too little connected to the aspects of life in you. The road to your deepest Self leads *through the soul*. It goes down in a spiral to the deepest point and from there up again. This means that you, a man, begin in the layer of your abstract thought but then—through the fall into your soul—land in the area of emotions and feelings, developing those facets which belong to it. Only then will it be possible for you not only to think clearly but also to feel and experience things from the inside, thus really connecting to yourself. In this way, you become, as Jung calls it, more 'whole'. This in turn opens the path to yet deeper-lying powers and intuitions of the Spirit, your spiritual Self. You gradually develop the powers that belong to phases 5 and 6. These take you, as the example of Stephan Peijnenburg shows, to a completely new relationship to the world around you.

The woman's road through the seven phases

Phase 2: The old group
As a girl, you also fully belong to groups in this phase, for instance your family, friends and clubs which have a certain influence on you. This influence is much stronger than in the case of boys, because of the workings of the

centrifugal force. As we already saw, a woman has an open awareness that works from the centre outwards towards the surroundings and wishes to enfold them. As a girl, you are therefore strongly focused on your surroundings, the relationships you have with people and the feelings you have about them. This focus can be so strong that for much of the time you are busy meeting other people's needs, and putting your own aside. You are also very sensitive to how others relate to you and how they feel about you. It shows how dependent you are on others in this period.

All these elements, together with the fact that the centripetal, concentrating force does not in the first instance work as strongly as in a boy or man, lead to your difficulty, as a growing woman, in finding yourself. You see yourself through the eyes of others. This can be a positive picture if you conform to their expectations but it can also be a more negative one. Girls and women have a 'relational self', as it is called in psychology. That is a feeling of self, or ego, which exists mainly as a relationship to others. Add to this relational self-feeling the fact that a woman's 'I' has its roots mainly in the soul, in the feelings and emotions where everything is constantly changing and in motion, and you will understand that her self-awareness or ego is at first far less strong than that of a man. Things can be 'this way' but the next moment 'that way'.

Phase 3: The 'I'-person

It is therefore not surprising that the process of individualization which makes you a person in your own right does not run as smoothly for a woman as it does for a man. Men are supported in this process by their strong link to their physical body and the centripetal force working in it.

Not having this support, women have to experience this

awareness of their own centre in another way. Their natural propensity, with its accent on the centrifugal forces of
the soul, actually prevents this process of individualization
at first. This is often aggravated by their surroundings. A
girl should, after all, according to tradition, be sweet and
kind, adaptable and self-effacing, and definitely not have
an obvious ego. That is the way you usually behave.
Nowadays, there are mothers who see this pattern and
stimulate their daughters to stand up for themselves and
be more assertive, in other words, to show more ego-
characteristics. On the other hand, this sometimes leads to
forced behaviour.

Of course, it is not so that a growing girl has no
centralizing awareness at all. Of course she has. The centripetal force which is so strong in men also works in you as
a woman, just as the centrifugal force acts in men—in the
background. This concentrating force makes you able to
centre your awareness, think and make decisions at school
and in your work. These are activities which strengthen
your self-awareness. But, because of your centrifugally
focused awareness, this does not happen in the same way
as in a man. If a man forms an opinion or reaches a conclusion about something, he does so fairly quickly on the
basis of what he already knows. Then he tests his view-
point by announcing it firmly. The reactions he gets allow
him to evaluate its worth and maybe alter his opinion.

A woman first collects a lot of information and then
weighs up the various points of view. During that process,
you want to talk about it with others, not in order to adopt
their viewpoints but because you only gain clarity yourself
from the exchange of ideas. Even when you have formed
an opinion and have even stated it, you are, in contrast to a
man, open to other suggestions. For instance, you say: 'It

seems to me that ... but what do you think?' You always try to retain the connection to your surroundings.

Phase 4: The transformation

The crisis of the transformation phase also manifests itself to a woman gradually, by way of inner stress, insecurity and, in particular, by a feeling of emptiness and estrangement from herself. You feel that something must be done, but what? In general, a woman is not so overcome by emotions as a man in this phase. You are, after all, by nature more at home in the second layer of your soul, that of feelings and emotions. It is not a strange area to you. You are more distressed by the feeling of the inner chaos in your soul and the experience of being stuck in that layer and not knowing where to go. Recurring questions in this period are: Who am I really? What have I come for? What is my mission or task in life?

Here too, unexpected events often trigger the crisis and force you to reflect, to start working on yourself and take steps. For instance, your partner falls in love with someone else, you lose your job and nice colleagues through reorganization or your relationship runs aground, you become ill, or whatever.

In this transformation phase, women, too, often call in the help of a coach, a therapist or, for instance, a course in self-management in order to change from focusing on the emotional dependence on the surroundings to connection to the ego. What do *I* want, irrespective of what others think? What are the needs and longings in my own life? What do I want to achieve? What characteristics or powers do I need for that? What do I need to do?

In this reflective phase, you become conscious of your strong and weak sides, you work on unsolved problems and dependence from the past and you take your male focus as an example for concentration on where your life is going. Many women make a new start in this period. They start training for something, set up their own business, apply for a higher function, thus becoming economically less dependent on the surroundings. A woman who took a managerial post in a large concern said:

> These past few years I have been able to keep myself, for the first time in my married life. I am no longer dependent on Fred. And let me tell you, I never again will be. I shall see to that, whatever happens. Before, when things were difficult between us, I used to think: My God, what would I do without him? And I didn't only mean emotionally. I mean, I know I am emotionally dependent on him. But the great difficulty was the financial dependence and the terrible fear this caused.[17]

For her, financial independence helped her to become increasingly free from her surroundings emotionally and to develop her own sense of self and self-esteem.

Strengths and weaknesses in men and women

What do the above sketches of the road of a man and that of a woman through the various phases show? A man's strength lies in his centric, intellectual awareness, which makes him clear, determined and purposeful, able to make decisions on the basis of facts and arguments and fulfil his task. His weakness is that he is insufficiently aware of the needs of the people around him, does not take them into account or involve them in his choices. The intellectual, centripetal force of awareness makes him clear and objective on the one hand; on the other, it is often coupled to a certain unawareness or insensibility towards the emotions and feelings involved, the subjective element, in himself. The transformation period in phase 4 awakens him to this one-sidedness and provides him with the possibility of as yet developing his additional, female, qualities, which help him to connect to himself and to others. This not only enriches himself but also creates a great feeling of freedom. He is no longer stuck within an unconscious and fixed pattern but can choose freely how he wants to deal with people, things and situations.

A woman's strength lies in her sympathetic relationship with the people around her. She knows what their needs are and wants to take them into account or deal with them. Her weakness is that she easily gets carried away and then often goes too far. The reason is that she cannot distance herself enough from her surroundings. Her weakness is the tendency to become so involved in the needs and feelings of others that she forgets herself. She loses herself in the contact as such and does not learn enough to be able to stand firmly in herself and her surroundings. Another consequence of this attitude is that she wants to impinge too much on someone else's life, thus overstepping borders. The period of reflection in phase 4 and the ensuing road help her to conquer her one-sidedness by not only developing her female qualities but also her male ones, such as taking distance, analysing, making specific decisions, clarity, daring to make choices and defending frontiers. Many women who have gone through phase 4 say that only after the transformation process and the development of their own thinking and self-awareness did they feel a real connection to their being as a woman.

Catching up on neglected areas

What are you actually doing when, as a woman, you finally develop your male qualities? Let us have another look at how a woman goes through the different phases. Your strong orientation and dependence on your surroundings keep you in phase 2 longer than a man. It is difficult for your ego to cut loose from other people. This means that in phase 3, you do not really become an independent, free-standing person. Your development does go further but is largely based on subjective feelings. In other words, the strength that belongs to phase 3 — the 'I'-consciousness — has not been fully developed. Then you reach phase 4, the transformation phase. Reflection makes you aware of your strengths and qualities, but also of your female weaknesses and one-sidedness. You realize you will never really be able to be Yourself if you do not become more whole.

You therefore decide to develop your male side too. To be able to do this, you have partially to *return* to phase 3, the ego-phase, where, from your centred awareness, you can still develop those qualities and skills you will need along the road to phases 5, 6 and 7. This teaches you to think objectively and clearly, to aim at what you want to achieve, to stop being influenced by what others think of you or expect of you. You learn to say 'no'. You do not despair if things are not going so well; you do not mind if others do not like you. You no longer go back on a road once decided upon, even if you realize that others do not agree with it. In short, you determine your own goals, mark out the route towards achieving them and bring your contribution to the world. During this period, a woman is allergic to starting on relationships in which this newly won strength and freedom have no place or could be endangered. Some women therefore consciously avoid new relationships for a time in order not to disturb this process of becoming independent.

How does a man go through the various phases? In phase 2, you cut loose from your surroundings fairly quickly and develop your ego. You extract everything possible from phase 3. You become independent and no longer feel dependent on your surroundings. You enjoy your own strength.

Through phase 4, however, the transformation phase, you become aware of your one-sidedness as a man and as yet decide to develop your undeveloped female side. Here again, you have to go *back*, in this case to phase 2, the phase in which you still felt linked to your surroundings. While a woman must take an inner hold of herself and come out, the man's task is to turn inward and attune to his own soul. You must therefore return to the vulnerable, emotional parts of yourself which remained at the stage of phase 2 but which, when developed, you will need if you want to deal with other people in a new way. In general, this period is one of insecurity and vulnerability for the man—fear too. Through this turning to his own soul, he is afraid of losing his independence and again becoming dependent on others, in particular his wife. One man described his fear thus:

Judy and I are very close; I do not experience this with anyone else. She often even knows what I am thinking. But that can be difficult. I mean, sometimes I am glad she knows me so well; it is reassuring and gives one a feeling of security. But sometimes I feel: ... I must leave her before she swallows me up, or something. I know it sounds silly, but that is what it feels like. I don't know why, but I then feel like a frightened little boy. But what am I afraid of? I wish I knew![18]

It is clear that, as a man, you must understand this fear and give it a place in your life. If you do not, your relationship with your partner is endangered.

In this phase, some men decide to work less and, for instance, look after the children in order to develop their own soul. Many fall in love and have a (short) relationship with another woman. Altogether, in this phase there is a great need for contact with women. This need leads to confusion if it is not properly understood. Why is it so strong? Because a man in this stage has a special need for soul contacts. Through soul contacts one can grow. As a matter of course, you look for this in contacts with women. Ego-centred men cannot help you. Many men going through this phase also greatly dislike men with macho behaviour. They can hardly stand it. But since the need for internalizing your feelings is so strong, your contact with women may again make you dependent and this breeds insecurity. Because: Am I not delivering myself into her hands? Will this not push me back to phase 2, in which I lose my ego? It is clear that much understanding and wisdom is demanded of women in this situation. In the contact with a man in this phase, they must always ask themselves whether their attitude and behaviour free him or make him dependent on her. By ever asking this question, a woman becomes aware of her own subjective and manipulative sides. This awareness forces her to make choices. This, in turn, leads to self-knowledge and a more objective and moral attitude.

Development continues

In the processes in and around phase 4, you can also get stuck in different phases. As a man, you can get stuck in the ego-phase, in the transformation phase and in the emotional phase. During this catching-up period, you can, for instance, get the feeling that you have 'succeeded' if you are able to show your emotions and can deal with those of others.

The phase you return to is, however, always temporary. The aim is to carry on from there.

The next step is that you learn to integrate your feelings, and your sensitivity towards the questions and needs of others and yourself, into your personality, using your already existing male qualities.

The same principle applies to women. They can get stuck in the dependence of phase 2, in the transformation phase and, finally, in the egocentric concentration on themselves. They, too, must realize that the ego-phase, for instance, is an intermediate one, which, together with their female qualities, offers opportunities for growth to a higher level.

In this way, both men and women gradually develop those qualities which belong to the phases 5, 6 and 7.

PART TWO: SOCIAL DEVELOPMENT

6. Collaboration in an Architects' Office

Karin van den Hoven is 41 and Caroline de Grave 38 when they decide to work together. Both are architects.

Karin worked for years in a large architects' office. Five years ago she started on her own, using the extension on her house as an office.

Caroline also began her career as an architect in an office with several partners. She left to study in Italy, travelled around in the Mediterranean and returned to the Netherlands when she started on a relationship.

Karin has a family with three children. Caroline's relationship foundered. She is now on her own, has no children. She and Karin met while studying in Delft. They got on well together at the time.

While visiting old friends after her return to the Netherlands, Caroline also went to see Karin. Enthusiastically she tells her about new developments in architecture and the experiences she had. She is looking for somewhere to put these to good use.

Caroline's enthusiasm greatly appeals to Karin and tentatively she suggests they might work together. She has found that working on one's own has its disadvantages. To her surprise, she discovered that she missed the exchange of ideas and contact with a colleague. Caroline is interested. A small office is compact and flexible and that appeals to her. Further talks follow and they decide to give it a try. Their office will remain in Karin's house but, as soon as they have the means, they will buy premises together. They will each have their own clients but also do projects together. Artistically they complement each other very well.

The beginning of a partnership

On 1 April 1995, their partnership begins. They enjoy the contact with each other and the possibilities opened up by this new collaboration. Caroline contributes her experience and insight from recent years and Karin is responsible for the joint projects and does the planning. Karin comes alive and becomes enthusiastic for new experiments. They also meet at home and regularly go out for a meal together. Caroline finds a new partner and feels very happy with all these developments. Her new ideas are popular and she has plenty of work. Several big commissions come their way and the office flourishes. While Karin works from her office as far as possible, Caroline is often out. She spends a great deal of time with her clients, getting her inspiration from talking to them a lot and eating and drinking with them. Since this often involves late nights, she is regularly late coming into the office or does not appear at all. Karin and the part-time secretary then have to field all sorts of things for her. Karin becomes increasingly irritated by this, the more so since Caroline accepts a great many commissions but has difficulty in finishing them on time. This means that many loose ends are left. If there is one thing Karin hates, it is people who do not keep their side of the bargain. She tries to curb her annoyance but it does not always work. She does not want to nag. Things are going well, after all, and she is afraid that complaints will destroy their collaboration.

Caroline reacts to Karin's remarks by promising to do better next time. She does for a time but then there is another lapse.

Disagreement

When Caroline has again spent a great deal of money on what she calls public-relations activities, this is too much for thrifty Karin. The bomb bursts. She is furious because Caroline is risking their partnership. When Karin's fury is spent, they manage to talk it over. They decide to have the secretary work a day more, agree to have a meeting every Monday and also on some other things. This structure helps and Caroline can more or less manage to stick to it. She still comes in late regularly, but Karin decides to let this go.

Their relationship, however, has altered somewhat. They do not get together so often and hardly have exciting discussions any more. The meetings are purely businesslike. Their relationship has cooled and the distance between them seems bigger. Caroline wants to buy new premises for their office. Karin hesitates. Something stops her but she does not know exactly what. Caroline insists. Karin talks to her husband about it. She then admits to herself that she is bitterly disappointed. A female colleague with whom she discusses the problem advises her to talk to Caroline but she feels she cannot. What if Caroline is hurt by what she says and leaves? No way! She decides to act as normally as possible and to postpone the decision on the new premises for as long as she can.

The crisis

Then Caroline's partner is involved in a serious road accident and dies. Caroline collapses and takes sick-leave. Karin visits her and tries to comfort her but does not know how. For the first time, Caroline totally shuts herself off from her. They get little further than an exchange of platitudes.

Caroline goes to a therapist and, after some time, to a careers-coach. She wants to know where to go from here, both in her personal life and in her work. Everything has fallen apart. One item in her recovery-plan is an evaluation with Karin, chaired by the coach. Both are initially scared of it, but once they are sitting opposite each other and the coach makes his introductory remarks, they start talking. How has our relationship been up to now? What have I felt about you? And you about me? Both put their anger and disappointment into words. Unfulfilled expectations are revealed, inspiring moments highlighted. What do we share? This leads to the question: Do we want to carry on together? How do we want to do this? What would then have to change in ourselves and in our work-relationship?

A different future

The result of this talk and those that follow is the decision to continue their collaboration, but in a different way. Their mutual contact must now be the pivot and they want to recover its inspirational effect. Since they both lack the communicative skills necessary for this, they decide to enlist the help of another coach and work on it together. They hear that there are at least two important aspects to a good (work-) relationship. The first is that collaboration is always a process, and the second that real contact demands a certain way of communicating.

The coach explains that a process of collaboration usually begins in an atmosphere of enthusiasm, in which the partners experience each other positively and feel related. Sooner or later, however, this stage is followed by a period in which they feel opposed to each other and can hardly reach the other, if at all. If this phase is ignored or not understood, the problems increase and often eventually lead to the end of the collaboration or relationship.

Building the bridge

Caroline and Karin realize that their collaboration up to now has gone through these stages. They are glad they can gain control of the situation by recognizing and classifying it. Next they learn how they can regain contact with each other in a new way. They must learn to express their thoughts, opinions and especially their feelings. And to ask each other questions, such as: I see you are irritated. Can you tell me what you feel and think? And then to go on asking and listening to what the other has to say until you understand what she means. This must be put into words, summarized and checked whether it is right. If it is, a bridge is built and a new connection with the other is created. The other feels she has been heard and recognized and this gives her a feeling of relief and liberation, and — curiously enough — also of inner strength. At the same time, something happens between the partners. Often they look at each other, keep quiet for a moment and then smile or nod at each other.

A new bond

Caroline and Karin found that by learning to talk to each other in this conscious way, they developed a new sort of bond—one in which they learnt to accept and deal with their intrinsic differences and the difficulties that arose from them. They also discovered how important it was to reflect on themselves, in particular on their own feelings and behaviour—What do I feel? Why do I say that?—and then classifying, gaining insight and asking: How can I deal with this in the right way?

Karin and Caroline's enthusiasm and mutual inspiration returned, but in an entirely different way. It seemed, they said, as if they only now saw and got to know and appreciate the other. Finally, they both expressed their happiness with the insight this difficult and often laborious process had given them.

7. The Development of Relationships and Groups in Seven Phases

Relationships between people—and thus also groups—develop in stages, just as the individual does. As shown in Caroline and Karin's collaboration process, this goes through different phases. There is a period of enthusiasm, one in which differences come to the fore and a crisis phase. There are even more. If one looks closely, one sees that relationships between people run through the same stages as the individual goes through. They may have different names but essentially they are the same. It makes no difference whether the relationship is between people who live together, work together or have a lot to do with each other.

As with the individual, it is important to recognize the different phases in order to understand and be able to deal with the group-process properly. The phases which human relationships and groups go through are as follows.

Phase 1: Undivided unity

'Everybody has a memory of a place where all is whole and one. The desire for security in something complete remains with us all our lives.' This statement by the Swiss psychologist Julia Onken[19] contains a great deal of truth. To a greater or lesser degree, there is in each of us the wish to return to the original security and unity from which we came. This wish plays a role in all our relationships with other people. Something in us wants to fully unite with the other and so return to the greater whole of phase 1. As I indicated before, however, there is at the same time something in us that resists this. That is our 'I', the most personal part of us. The struggle between the two, between merging with the greater whole and the need to be yourself, plays a crucial role in our development.

Phase 2: The old group

In phase 2, you identify not so much with the greater whole as with a group of people or another person in whom you lose yourself. Some people feel that this happens when they take part in family celebrations or reunions, where they unconsciously take on 'a different colour', act differently from who they really are, in order to belong to the 'old group'. Another example: people who identify so strongly with the company for which they work that they *are*, in a certain sense, that company. The characteristics of phase 2 are most apparent when people are in love. Especially when that feeling is mutual, they lose themselves in each other. When you are in love, you want to see a lot of the other person, stay close to them and do a lot together. It does not matter much what. The one lives, as it were, for the other.

A similar situation can be seen, in a calmer, more modified form, when people start working together through enthusiasm. This can be seen in the example of Karin and Caroline. They are enthusiastic about each other, both as people and as professionals, and about the possibilities which will arise from collaboration.

Characteristic of this phase is that you identify mainly with the positive things that you have in common. During this period you are nice to each other and always present your best side. Common ground is emphasized, individual differences get less attention, are put aside or even denied. Bumps are overlooked, irritations not voiced and quarrels and conflicts hardly occur. In other words, there is a positive exchange, in which you confirm many things. For many people who live or work together, this phase is proof that you really can be happy together and live and work in harmony.

Phase 3: The 'I'-person

The struggle
Sooner or later—sometimes after two months, sometimes after a year or two—the situation changes and the next phase sets in. It is, for instance, heralded by one (or both) partner(s) suddenly making their own plans and doing things in which the other has no part or which they are actually against. But it can also come about by differences of opinion, irritations and quarrels. You become irritated by the mess on the other's desk, by appointments which are not kept, by the mobile phone which is not shut off during meals or a meeting and so on. In this phase, you allow yourself to become conscious of the other's failings or weaknesses and the way in which they annoy you. The original enthusiasm turns into disappointment, because the idyll of phase 2 has been disturbed. You accuse the other of untidiness, unreliability, not taking others into account. They in turn have a thing or two to say about you and a quarrel ensues. Or you keep quiet and vent your anger by sabotage, showing your sadness or not speaking to the other. In this way you try to convince the other that

their behaviour is wrong and needs to change, namely, to your way of thinking.

Disappointment and assertiveness

Two things characterize phase 3 in relationships and groups. One is that you are angry or disappointed that the other, by being unexpectedly different, has disturbed the harmony. The other is that you assert your ego by telling the other — often with the best intentions — what to do. This could be 'helping' the other with your solution to their problem. You say what you would do if you were in their shoes. Or you want to change them so that they think and act differently. Or convince them that you are right and they are not.

You also see this tendency in collaboration situations such as a city council or a management team, where people try to push their own ideas and plans without taking those of others into consideration.

Thus in this phase, individual differences come to the fore. In contrast to phase 2, you do not try to hide them. You face up to them, but with a difference. You now want to wipe out the differences between you so that everything returns to normal and harmony is restored, at least according to your view of the matter.

Phase 3 is the ego-phase, the phase of conflict and struggle with each other. Who will be boss? Whose ideas or values will predominate? Who is the leader and who the follower? Where the one, where the other? The struggle in this phase has to do with determining precedence in the relationship, in the team or in the group. Instead of the feeling of belonging, as in phase 2, you now confront the other, weighing them up, judging who is the strongest or shrewdest, who has or wants to have the most power.

Meanwhile, you build a wall around yourself in order to feel strong and powerful and make yourself invulnerable. Phase 3 is obviously the ego-phase in the relationship.

Chaos
Phase 3 is a very chaotic one because you are usually unable to fathom the process or deal with it. You experience conflict, disappointment, incapacity, estrangement, coolness and distance. This makes those involved despair. They realize they are growing apart but do not know how to deal with each other or how to move on. In the collaboration between Caroline and Karin, this dilemma was obvious. Phase 3 is the phase of disintegration, the process in which the former unity, the former bond is split into smaller parts, cliques, splinter-groups or separate individuals.

The diagram on page 36 clearly shows this process. Many relationships, but also joint ventures such as societies or political parties, come to an end at this stage. The differences of opinion are irreconcilable. You see that you do not have the same aims or the same ideas about the aims and in the end the only thing to do is to separate. The next step is to look for another partner or to carry on as a splinter-group and form a new society or political party. Usually the process in phases 2 and 3 is then repeated.

Organization and negotiation
Another clear characteristic of the social interaction in this phase is that a need for form and structure is felt. One reason for this is that you realize that things do not happen by themselves. Expectations that the other will do something or come up with a solution are not met and lead to irritation. On the other hand, you try to stem and

control the growing chaos in human relationships by means of better organization. Thus people who live or work together arrive at a more concrete division of labour at this stage, formulate the responsibilities of each and reach new agreements. Karin and Caroline, for instance, agreed on regular meetings, had the secretary work an extra day and so on. In this way, you attempt to get the problems under control. To some degree, this works. The new structure makes for clarity and makes life more worth living and more pleasant. Besides, it keeps the partners and the members of the team together — for the time being.

Characteristic for most of the agreements made at this stage by those involved is the wish for an equal division of the pluses and minuses. If one does this, the other does that. Division of labour is negotiated. Many people assume that there is an unwritten law which says that for everything you do you should get some return. This principle of balance and negotiation comes up again if people consciously tackle the conflicts which arise in this phase. The question then asked is: how can we deal with each other in a way that produces no winners or losers, which would only re-ignite the problems or crises in this ego-phase, but that there are only winners? The attempt towards a so-called win-win-situation forms the basis for the modern method of dealing with conflict: mediation. It is used when the partners or group are still together, but also if they have already separated and need to settle all sorts of practical things.

Getting stuck and regression
By far the most collaborations, groups and relationships get no further than this phase 3 and get stuck. This can also

be seen in politics. The battle for position and power is fought in many ways. These are characterized by a great many set patterns of behaviour and reaction by all sorts of structures, rules and unwritten agreements which govern the current values. The result is that the main focus is on rules and habits and not on the mutual possibilities for growth. This type of behaviour is the most prevalent in our society today.

Some people cannot stand the chaos in phase 3 and regress, partially or entirely, to the previous state, phase 2. The norm then is being nice and kind to each other and on no account permit any conflicts. The unwritten rule is: say or do nothing which could hinder or offend the other. If another hurts, bores or irritates you, pretend not to notice or care. Change the subject as soon as you can. In other words, the differences of opinion and irritation are repressed and go underground. There they have negative effects, cause tension and sooner or later lead to an explosion.

Such regression, from phase 3 to phase 2, is always at the expense of the individual development of one or both partners or of the members of a group or team because, besides the individuality of the participants, honesty and intimacy are also destroyed. As in phase 3, the relationship has no future in phase 2. The living element decreases, boredom reigns and in the end the relationship ceases.

Phase 4: The transformation

How do partners or groups progress from phase 3 to 4, and from there to 5 and 6? The transformation of phase 4 begins when, feeling dissatisfied, unfulfilled or desperate in phase 3, you acknowledge that you want to continue with the

other(s) and look for insight, but at the same time realize
that you do not know the way and lack the necessary skills.
Knowing that you do not know and are incompetent is to
recognize your *impotence*. A great medieval genius, Nicolaus Cusanus, already pointed out that this realization
paves the way to finding the truth. 'The more we have
become knowledgeable and wise in this ignorance, the
nearer we are to the truth,' he wrote in 1440.[20]

Impotence

The transformation of phase 4 sets in when you, as partner
or as a member of a team, voice your feelings of despera-
tion and incompetence – of impotence – and put a name to
them. Without laying the blame on the other(s), you say
how you feel in a certain situation and what sort of problems or resistance this generates in you. You speak for
yourself, using the personal 'I'. By making yourself vulnerable in this way, you get closer to yourself. The door to
your real, deeper Self, which resides in feelings, is opened
and you say things you would never have thought possible
in earlier stages. People who speak from this deeper layer
become 'real' and authentic and, strangely enough, actually emanate strength in their impotence. Partners or team
members who approach each other like this and give each
other opportunity to voice their frustrations, fears, difficulties or pain make for a very special atmosphere, characterized by openness, trust, security, interest,
understanding and involvement. One could say, of honesty and love. This shows that completely different forces
are at work amongst them than in the previous phases.
Honesty, love, understanding, trust and involvement are
spiritual forces that are able to connect people to each other
in a completely new way. Spiritual forces integrate sepa-

rate individuals into a whole, a new group. One could also say, a new sort of community in which everyone's individuality has a place and from there contributes in its own unique way to the greater whole.

The conditions

Such a break-through in a collaboration or relationship, however, does not come about by itself. To make it possible, two important conditions must be met. The first is that at least one of those involved must have the courage to present themselves as vulnerable and speak out. The second is that the other(s), by their inner stance of involvement and attentive interest, give them the space to do so. There are conditions for this too.

The first is that, as listener, you recognize that the other is not only different from you, but actually a stranger, one, however, whom you can get to know and understand.[21] The second is that the other can only speak freely if you, the listener, can step out of the world of your own experiences and self-focus and into that of the other. In other words, if you can open yourself inwardly to the other and, by listening and asking questions, try to understand what they are saying. Through this inner attitude of listening and questioning, the other will be able to undergo and feel their experiences anew and thus gain insight and understanding. By doing so, the experiences are digested and absorbed. Then an inner strength is released. This inner strength is, in fact, nothing but the strength of the spiritual Self that develops in the other's ego and which conquers the inner incompetence or impotence.[22]

Rudolf Steiner formulated this process of transformation of a feeling of incompetence or impotence into strength very well. He said, 'It is often difficult for us to find words for our deepest feelings. But if there is someone who listens attentively and with respect, the speaker's tongue is loosened. Then there is trust, and truth can be found. This leads to a feeling of strength in the soul where before there was impotence. It is this feeling of strength that the other is seeking.'[23]

In doing this, not only the speaker but also the active listener connect to their inner, spiritual selves. And not only that. The strange thing is that then they also become connected in a new, deep and free way. That is what Karin and Caroline eventually discovered.

In practice, the task of dealing with each other in such a profound way in phase 4 proves to be a difficult one for many people and often founders if the necessary skills and capabilities are not developed. Many teams and partners recognize their incompetence in this area and call in the help of a coach or therapist or follow courses for schooling in communication and cooperation.

Conquering the ego

Phase 4 is about conquering the ego, though not by negating or repressing it, as is customary in many eastern-orientated beliefs, but, by realizing how your ego works, consciously reining in these forces and learning to deal with them differently. In this way, you open your ego, your everyday self, and reshape it from within. The transformation process in phase 4 means that you, as an individual, must discover and consciously learn to use your own strengths, your developed sides and your qualities. Besides this, you must dare to see and work on your weaknesses, your incapacities and your imprisonment in your own ego. Only thus can you reach the deeper layers in yourself, awakening your spiritual 'I', your spiritual Self.

The same is true of your ability to be a listening partner for him/her with whom you have a relationship or for the other members of the group. In your contacts with others, you must also learn to be conscious of your ego-aspirations and learn to deal with them and reshape them. In order to do this, you must see to it that you do not lose yourself entirely in the other but also remain within yourself. You should not stand critically opposite the other, but stand next to them. And then, by opening your heart and immersing yourself in the feelings, thoughts and behaviour of the other, empathizing with them, you try to understand the other from their point of view. Scott Peck here uses the word, 'offering'.[24] Up to now, in phases 2 and 3, you have indulged your own ego-feelings in your contacts with other people. There was as yet no question of true perception or really getting to know the other. In everything you experienced in your relationship with the other, you experienced yourself in particular and in the first place. In phase 4, your eyes are opened to this fact with a shock, waking you up. You want to learn to do this differently. You want to learn how to deal with and curb your own one-sidedness and egocentricity and to develop abilities which help the other to come forward and be able to contribute something of their own. That is what Scott Peck means by 'offering' your ego: rejecting the continual indulging of your own ego-aspirations which make you feel so good and developing the objective, giving strengths in yourself. As everything in phase 4, this demands insight and therefore awareness and conscious choices and implementation.

You then discover how valuable personal differences and contributions are in the relationship or collaboration, however difficult these may be to deal with. The other's being different and their contribution now becomes a goal in itself — a source of research and insight, practice and inspiration and thus of personal and spiritual growth.

Inner awakening
Phase 4 is all about consciousness and steering from your 'I', both in relation to yourself and your relationships with other people. You observe yourself and resolve, by means of your conscious will and control, to work on yourself and your qualities in relation to other people. The means you use for the development of this consciousness is reflection.

You reflect on yourself, on others and the relationship with others. You observe, you feel what another person feels and what you feel, you gain insight, learn, make choices, change things or confirm them and then let them go. I will say more about this process of reflection in chapter 9.

Through this inner activity, this constant process of observing, questioning, searching, deciding, implementing, bringing into practice and learning from it, you become a more conscious person. That is to say: your spiritual Self is awakened and becomes active in you. Your inner strength grows. You notice that you feel freer, more creative, more honest and more involved. In short, you become more your Self. This leads to your being there for others in an increasingly all-embracing, freer and more conscious way, able to give them what they need.

Phase 5: The spiritual Self

It will by now be clear that spiritual development is primarily a personal thing. From phase 2 through phase 4, while going through your own transformation process, you are mainly focused on yourself and your own devel-

opment and not so much on the other and their individuality and needs. This is why we have so many social
problems nowadays in our relationships and collaboration
with other people. In phase 5, too, you are still engrossed in
your own personal and spiritual development. It could not
be otherwise. In order to be able to build up new, i.e., free
relationships, you first have to become self-sufficient
spiritually as well. You must be reflective, have the skills to
gain insight and be able to manage yourself and your own
life. In other words, you must practise personal leadership.
This, too, is a characteristic aspect of the development of
your spiritual Self in phase 5.

Personal leadership
Personal leadership has been described as a road to
development by which you become increasingly responsible for your own choices, behaviour, results and well-
being. With part of our personality, with its ego-character,
still living in phases 2 and 3, we are dependent and reactive. If others treat you well, you feel well. If not, you
become defensive. If it is sunny, you feel fine. If the
weather is bad, you achieve less. Reactive, dependent
behaviour means that your feelings and your life are
determined by others or by the circumstances.

Steven Covey, in his book *The Seven Habits of Highly
Effective People*,[25] shows that such a reactive stance leads to
an extra problem, namely, that you are also dependent on
the moods and shortcomings of others — become imprisoned. He points out that people in any situation,
however constrained and however dependent they are, are
always able to choose how to deal with it. We can always
ask ourselves: Do I let myself be governed by the bad
weather or am I going to do my work well? Do I let my

working life be spoilt by another, or do I choose not to? This is called a pro-active stance. Pro-active means that you know you have a choice and can consciously make use of it.

Covey cites the example of a hospital nurse under a nagging manager. This manager is always finding fault, ignores her and never praises her. Up to now, the nurse's response had always been reactive. The man made her life a misery and she always took her frustration home with her. After hearing a lecture by Covey, she realized that she had actually chosen to be miserable up till then. Remaining in such a situation is also a question of choice, though an unconscious one. Now she realized that she could choose to handle the situation differently and not suffer from his behaviour. Once she had seen that, the bits of the puzzle fell into place. She suddenly felt freer. The nurse: 'I felt as if I had been sentenced to death and had suddenly been set free. I wanted to shout as loudly as possible: "I am free!" I will not let myself be dominated by one man's moods any longer!'[26]

The difference between reactive and pro-active behaviour is that, in the former, you let your reactions be determined by other people and situations, in the latter by what you yourself consider important. What you consider important is always the result of certain principles or values. In the example of the nurse, the principle was that she no longer wished to be dominated by the moods of one man. In that of the weather, it was the value of wanting to produce good work. In phase 4 and the following ones, the important thing is to transform your reactive behaviour into pro-active behaviour. It is no longer the surroundings, but your own principles and values which govern the motives for your behaviour. Principles and values are qualities of your spiritual Self. By becoming conscious of this and thus making choices on how to deal with other people, situations and yourself, you awaken these spiritual forces.

Pro-activity and collaboration

In collaboration with others, too, the question of reactive and pro-active behaviour is always a factor. One often hears people say: 'I'm not given enough space.' What they are really saying is: 'Because of the other, I cannot come into my own' — a pure example of reactive behaviour. I put my contribution and even my own development into the hands of the other and take no responsibility for the situation myself.

If you become pro-active, you turn things round. Instead of being passive, you become active and take the initiative. You think about the problem and come up with a well-considered suggestion or plan. You ask yourself: how can I contribute positively in such and such a situation? Or: how can we solve this or that problem? You work out a concept solution and talk it over with your colleague. This is not to get approval or permission from the other, but to gear your ideas to those of the other and make choices jointly. Experience shows that the more pro-active people are in a collaboration situation, the more pleasant and fruitful this is.

Leader of yourself and your own destiny

Personal leadership and pro-activity lead to your making your own choices and knowing that nobody else is responsible for what you do or do not do. In other words, you yourself are responsible for the way in which you deal with your situation and surroundings, for your behaviour, the results in your life and work and, finally, for your well-being. In phase 5, we realize that we are the leader of ourselves and our own destiny.

What you decided to do in phase 4, you implement in phase 5.

Through reflection, you work on insight and change in yourself. You learn to recognize and deal with reaction patterns. You learn to know and use your own qualities. And you become aware of the values and principles that are important to you and that govern your life. These are the new, inner, points of reference that determine control over your own life and that with others.

Phase 6: The new community

In every form of collaboration or living together, two important aspects can be seen: the job or task that needs doing, and the people who have to do it together. The one is dependent on the other. If you put a group of people together, tell them what needs to be done and think everything will go smoothly by itself, you will soon be disappointed. People have all sorts of needs which must be met if they are to accomplish their task well. In particular, these needs are in the social sphere. The collaboration between Caroline and Karin in the architects' office demonstrated this. They finally become aware that they want to communicate well with each other, solve their problems and conflicts, understand the other and her background *and* move on personally and with each other. This shows that they want to grow.

In the terms of this book, one could also say: *within a relationship or collaboration, people have the intrinsic need for development through the various phases, both personally and in their mutual social relationship.* That means that there is a need for the new sense of community. Sometimes they even voice this longing.

How is this new community formed in this phase?

Difference between phase 6 and phase 2

It actually begins in the transformation phase. A partnership or team begins development in the sense of phase 6 when those involved are able to voice and share with the other(s) their feelings, worries, joys, victories, ideas, plans, needs, faults, wishes and so on. Sharing in such a way that others actively listen, empathize, think and try to understand, and thus gain insight into the questions and experiences of the other. If members of a group do this, experiences can be digested, essentials sought out, new ideas formed and lessons learnt, as I have already showed. This heals and gives strength — spiritual strength which makes one wiser and provides inner stability. The other members of the group are, as it were, the sounding-board for the consciousness process, the spiritual growth, of the individual.

It is now obvious what the important difference is between a group in phase 6 and one in phase 2. In the latter, the individual and the personal experiences of the individual have no role to play. Everything revolves around the group as a whole. In phase 6, on the contrary, the individual is central and the other members of the group put themselves at the disposal of that individual's development. In other words, a complete about-turn takes place between phase 2 and phase 6 — in fact in phase 4, the transformation phase. *The personal inner activity* of phase 4 causes the transformation of the ego and the awakening of the spiritual Self or the divine core. By thus turning inwards, the Self is awakened and the inner can again turn outwards.

The more you develop in this way, as an individual in relation to the others, the stronger you become inwardly. You gather courage and strength to develop new qualities and reach out to new experiences. This process, in which everyone contributes to each other's individual growth, also causes the members of the group to feel more strongly connected. Thus a community is born.

Workshop
In reality, the relationship, group or team in phase 6 is a workshop—a place where you work at something together. It could be compared to playing in an orchestra. There, each musician plays their own instrument in their own unique way. They then try to unite all these different, individual contributions into one large, musical whole. This does not happen by itself. You have to practice, individually and together, by trial and error. During this process, you become aware of how much depends on the quality of each member's contribution, the individual musicians, but also how dependent your contribution is on that of the other. If the harp-player does not come in at the right time and with the right tone, you, as a cellist, cannot contribute well either and vice versa.

The same situation as that in an orchestra can be found in a relationship or a team. Living or working together teaches you that not only is your own contribution to the collective task indispensable, but that of the others as well. You therefore have to see to it in this phase that each of the other members of the group can make their contribution. You create space for them and stimulate their contribution: 'I have not heard your opinion or ideas. What have you to

say?' Or: 'How would you do this?' Also you pay attention
to possible problems or obstacles in contributing which the
other may have, not by sweeping the problems under the
carpet, as in phase 2, or by confronting them with their
inability, as in phase 3, but by freely and objectively saying
what you see and experience. This can be coupled to asking
whether you can help in their process, for instance by
talking about it.

In phase 6, then, you become aware, as an individual and
as a member of a team, of your mutual dependence on each
other and you feel involved in the other, their contribution
and individual struggle, both professionally, personally
and socially.

As in an orchestra, work in a team or relationship is a
huge social task in which you are constantly confronted
with your own failings and those of others. You are continually practising. You are practising to become more
'human', in the true sense of the word, in relation to each
other.

Security

An important condition for a community such as in the
sense of phase 6 is that its members feel secure. When do
people feel secure? When there is no question of constant
competition and mutual rivalry, such as in phase 3, but a
communal wish for insight, honesty and objectivity. If the
ability to listen to each other and understand each other is
present, in phase 6 you can put away the armour of your
ego and be inwardly free towards each other. You are
enthusiastic about the differences, talents and strengths
that everyone has. You see the 'being different' not as a
danger or as competition, but as a supplement to yourself.
You accept each other's limitations, misconceptions, mis-

takes, wrong ideas and so on as a given. You continually try to open up and make yourself inwardly free for new views and for understanding the other. We see that here, too, there is always further development of consciousness and new skills and abilities to support this process. Without these, you cannot reach phase 6. As from phase 4, the strength of the spirit only develops against the current. This means that nothing happens of its own accord but that everything must be consciously won through one's own and communal effort.

Becoming yourself in a relationship

If the conditions for security have been met, you, as individual in the group, can speak from the heart, from your vulnerable side. You feel you are being listened to, that you are accepted as you are, that no one wants to change you, convert you, pin you down or convince you. You know that no one will use what you have said against you or confront you negatively. If there is such an atmosphere of openness and freedom, you can appear with all your frustrations, pain, ideas, guilt and aspirations. You can dispose of the walls and masks you created in the ego-phase and be entirely yourself.

Disagreement and conflict

Does this mean that in such a community people are only nice and kind to each other? Not in the least. Since differences between people are not pushed aside but are allowed to exist, there will, of course, be differences of opinion, disagreements and conflicts. However, in contrast to phase 3, you do not get bogged down by them but, in phase 6, are able to cope with all the differences of opinion because you understand them and can place them. You create space for healthy confrontation, but there are no quarrels to upset the living or working together. Besides, as individual and with the others, you learn to deal with conflicts in such a way that each team member feels understood and respected. This again implies further development of consciousness and practical action, otherwise you cannot move to phase 6 together.

Conquering the ego

Clearly, phase 6 demands two different abilities. Firstly, that you become aware of your egocentricity and your own ego-aspirations. And secondly, that you learn to observe and understand the other as he really is, with all his positive and negative qualities, possibilities and leanings. If you really want to see, hear and understand the other, to create space for him to speak, you must know yourself and always reopen or empty yourself inwardly to make the process with the other possible. Otherwise your own feelings and ego-aspirations will continually be in the way, so that you only hear yourself. This means that, in your contact with others, you must be aware of your own feelings, emotions, thoughts, impressions, ideas and motives. You must always be able to curb them and create openness towards the other. This inner emptying of your ego-aspirations, which want to make everything in you the same or subservient, is much more difficult than you think. Try listening to someone talking about something which is emotional for you and who has a completely different opinion from you. You will perceive that it is incredibly difficult to continue listening to the other, trying to realize what he means and to understand him. It takes a great deal of time and practice. Besides, we all have certain expectations of the other of which we are hardly even conscious.

Or presuppositions or prejudices are based on very short, limited experiences, and often turn out to be totally wrong. All these un-free attitudes limit or prevent our making real contact with the other and understanding him.

Many people experience a kind of pain when they learn to curb these ego-aspirations. The pain comes from having to give up something of the ego-feelings in order to make room for real contact with the other, which comes from another layer. So you really do 'offer' something when you learn to treat each other 'humanly', in the sense of phase 6. It is comforting to know that you get something very valuable in return: the experience of a trustworthy communal basis on which to build with each other.

Social abilities, forces from the spirit

It is obvious that you cannot make do with superficial relationship-techniques in phase 6. In order to recognize and deal with your ego-forces *and* to be able to make the step towards the other and to understand her or him, you need quite different abilities. As I already mentioned, these do not come from the ego but from the much deeper layers of your real Self, the spiritual core. There you find the forces that bring forth consciousness, insight and understanding and loving involvement with the other as part of the whole to which you too belong.

You can therefore say, with Stephen Covey, in an adapted form, that relationships in phase 6 are built from the core. In a relationship or collaboration, the most important thing is not what you know, say or do, but what you *are*.[27] That works. For the new community, you must be able to express something essential in yourself. You can only do this if you have personally gone through the transformation process in phase 4 and, as we have seen

earlier, have made the connection to your inner self in a
new way. From there, you can manage yourself and your
relationship with other people. That is to say, you need to
change from being reactive to being more and more pro-
active, and develop personal leadership — pro-activity and
personal leadership based on good, positive values and
principles to which you are true. Only then can you build
up a fruitful and longstanding relationship with others.

One could say that, on the road of your personal
development — in phases 4 and 5, the phases of
transformation and the development of the spiritual Self —
you create the conditions which make the new community
with others in phase 6 possible. Or, using the analogy of the
musicians in an orchestra, in phases 4 and 5, as individual
player, you work on yourself and your own instrument so
that you can make as good a contribution as possible to the
orchestra, the communal task, in phase 6.

Phase 7: Differentiated unity

The more you develop your skills individually as member
of an orchestra and the better you learn to play together
with the other musicians, concerned about the other as a
person and about their contribution, the more beautiful the
result will be. You become inspired, lifted above your own
individual limitations and, together with the other musicians, contribute to the realization of that beautiful
symphony. Here a unity is formed in cooperation, which is
more than the sum of the component parts. Nobody could
have played the symphony on their own. Nor would it
have come about had everyone just played their own part.
Only in the coordination and cooperation with all the

others does the beauty of the symphony sound in its full glory.

We could turn this round and say: the glorious performance of the symphony could only have taken place because individuals played their instruments well in their own way and, in collaboration with the other players, did that in such a way that everyone contributed with their specific skills to the realization of a new entity—the symphony. In this way, a differentiated unity develops: phase 7.

Through increased strength and productive creativity, a relationship or team can, in the same way as in an orchestra, contribute to the aims of the organization as a whole in an inspired way.

8. On the Way to a New Community

Other authors' group phases

The phases of development in relationships and groups, as hitherto described, are not entirely unique. They demonstrate a universal law which has also been discovered by others working with groups. The American B.W. Tuckman, for instance, in his book *Developmental Sequence in Small Groups*,[28] showed that a group develops in four phases from a collection of individuals into a strong cooperative unit. He called the phases: *forming, storming, norming* and *performing*. The fifth phase is then the farewell phase, *adjourning*. In the description of the phases storming, norming and performing, phase 3 of the previous chapter can be recognized. The forming phase, however, is different from what I described in phase 2 as 'the old group'. Both he and others describe this phase as follows:

> The individuals come together for the first time as a group. They are expectant. They first want to see how things work. Their main interest is in the social relationships and whether the situation is safe. This phase is sometimes called the *test-phase* or the *intellectual phase*. Talks are mainly about thoughts, more *about* themselves than *from* themselves. More personal contributions regarding feelings, emotions or wishes are held back or not admitted by the others. Irritations, too, remain unspoken and are curbed. The tendency is to compromise.

Thus the forming phase has both similarities and differences with phase 2, 'The old group', as described in the previous chapter. In both, irritation—negative emotions—are avoided and only come to the fore in the next phase. Where positive feelings towards each other predominate in phase 2 of the previous chapter, the predominant ones in *forming* are observation and thought. Both phase 2 as described by me and Tuckman's *forming* are part of the first stage in the formation of a relationship or group. Forming is mainly found in work or course situations where people meet for the first time. My phase 2 is found in situations where people find each other by themselves as a result of enthusiasm or love. One could say that the centripetal element dominates in the former and the centrifugal in the latter. This has to do with the difference between work and personal relationships. Both are followed by the developments I described for phase 3.

Ten Siethoff notes that many groups in our society already get stuck in this first phase, *forming*, without developing further.[29] This has far-reaching consequences, both in communes and in politics and economics. Since the relationships in these groups do not develop and deepen through further processes, the decisions made at this stage remain superficial. Problems are not tackled at the root, with all the resulting consequences.

It is interesting to note that the phases 4, 5 and 6, those of the spiritual element, are lacking in the vision of Tuckman and others. The formation of personal and group relationships stops in phase 3, the development of the 'I', when the group and its work have been structurally well organized and regulated. So they do not get beyond the ego-stage and control is mostly external.

In more than one phase at a time

In the development of relationships and groups, as in the individual's road, the different phases are not gone through one by one. In reality, they run into each other. At a certain point, one phase will predominate, but at the same time previous phases demand attention. In phase 3, for instance, when the members of a team feel they are individually separated and in opposition to each other, there may be a need to return to the harmonious atmosphere of phase 2 or even that of phase 1. Measures can be taken or agreements reached that lead back to this earlier stage. Parties with entertainers, dancing and drinks are organized, which give the feeling that the unity has returned again in some way. In itself, there is nothing against temporarily returning to an earlier phase and catching up on a missed piece of life. It is, however, important to realize when that happens and that you will have to return to phase 3 sooner or later.

Problems arise if such regression is made without insight and the rules and habits belonging to phase 2 are enforced on people as a matter of course: 'From now on we are only going to be nice to each other.' This however will soon give rise to opposition from those individuals who want to develop further in phase 3 and the phases that follow.

A complication is that in people who, personally or together, are living in phase 2, 3, 4, or 5, the ideals of phase 6, the new community, are already to be heard and want to be awakened. These unconscious ideals and aspirations make for expectations towards the other that cannot yet be met because the necessary conditions, such as seeing yourself objectively and empathizing with the other, are still missing. Thus, for example, you might, as a matter of course, expect the members of a group, mostly living in phase 3, to empathize with a problem you have and to understand you. The others could then throw you back on your own resources, saying that it is your problem and that you must solve it by yourself. It has nothing to do with them. This is a typical phase 3 reaction. I am I and you are you and everyone solves their own problems.

For the further growth of the team, group or relationship, it is important that everyone is conscious of the fact that there are always bits of development that get left behind and need to be 'fetched'. This is done by paying attention to things that point in that direction. For instance, when it turns out that differences of opinion are always being pushed away and disappear under the table. Or you notice an atmosphere of distrust and criticism which points to problems in phase 3.

Pseudo-community

A particular problem is that of groups and communities which think they are already in phase 6, the new community, while in practice the group shows more characteristics of phase 2 than of phase 6. This happens quite often in groups or communities that work or live together on the basis of high social, religious or spiritual ideals.

The idea that phase 6 has already been reached is an illusion. It is caused by the fact that everyone can envisage the ideal of a new type of relationships and a new community, but does not realize that the necessary conditions—empathizing and understanding the other as a distinct being and relinquishing the own ego-focus—have not yet been fulfilled.

Scott Peck, who worked with many groups and teams, discovered in his research that most of the groups that think they are in the phase of the real community (phase 6 in this book) are in fact living in what he calls the pseudo-community[30] (phase 2 in this book).

Getting stuck and regression

As has already been noted, a group can get stuck in any of the phases. In such cases, it tends to regress to a previous stage because the consciousness of the process it is in is lacking. This leads to the forces working in the previous phases pulling you back into an earlier stage.

Thus a group or relationship that is well on its way to phase 6, the new community, can quickly regress to phase 3 or even 2 if those involved do not reflect regularly on their personal and group functioning, evaluate it and grow and renew further. This is therefore another essential condition for life in phase 6.

Group members in different phases

The social situation in a relationship or group can become complicated if the phase some members are in is different from that of the group as a whole. It can happen that the group is already largely in phase 4 but that two members are personally still struggling with characteristics of phases 2 and 3 — freeing themselves from their surroundings and becoming conscious of their ego. These two can then hinder the group process. They put everything up for discussion, are critical or even cynical and in general do not make things easy. It is very important that together the reason for this conflict is found and consciously worked on. It is clear that the two people in phases 2 and 3 have different needs from the other members but these must be recognized if they are to take the next steps to join the others. A situation like this often occurs within teams and in partnerships.

In the same way, it can be difficult for an individual member, already in phase 5, to function in a team in which the ego-element of phase 3 is still dominant, so that the others are solely focused on their own achievements, prestige and success. The same is true of partnerships.

In short, it is quite a challenge to live or work together with partners or colleagues who are in another phase of development. Many conflicts and separations between people are caused by the fact that they are unable to recognize and understand the differences between them and the different phases they are in personally. If they were able to do this and mutually try to give each other the opportunity to develop in their own way, a good method of living and working together could be found.

The 'I'-phase

It is important to point out how essential phase 3, the development of the 'I'-person, the ego, is — not only for the individual, but also for the healthy development of relationships and teams. Without the development of the ego, you can never free yourself from your surroundings and become self-sufficient. This is an essential condition for the development of that most personal thing, the spiritual Self. Many people, however, find confrontation unpleasant and problematical. They therefore tend to revert to the needs and habits of phase 2, or, on the contrary, do not dare to go on to phase 3. This fear can be found in relationships and groups in which people desperately cling to the harmonious state of phase 2. Such people often get the advice to quarrel more often with each other, not so much for the quarrel in itself as for the recognition — phase 3 — that you are different individuals, each with their own process, stage of development, needs and colour. Another important aspect is that you realize that you must give each other space and freedom without thinking that this implicitly leads to not being able to find each other again, and estrangement. The developments described above show that this is always possible if the right conditions are fulfilled.

In his book *The Prophet*, the Lebanese writer and painter Kahlil Gibran strikingly put the challenge of phase 3, the conditions for further growth between people, into words. After recommending permitting the existence of spaces in togetherness, he says, in the chapter on marriage:[31]

Love each other, but do not make a bond of love; rather let it be an undulating sea between the shores of your souls.
Fill each other's cups, but do not drink from the same cup.
Give of your bread, but do not eat from the same piece.
Sing and dance together and be happy, but each alone, as are the strings of the lute, though the same music vibrates in them.
Give your hearts, but do not give them to each other in safekeeping.
For only the hand of life can hold your hearts.
And stand together, but not too close: for the pillars of the temple stand alone, and the oak and the cypress do not grow in each other's shade.

The ego-phase in female groups

The importance of phase 3, the ego-phase, also becomes clear if you study the functioning of female groups. On the surface, it often looks as if they bring quite a lot of phase 6 into practice. They talk a lot together and always pay attention to each other and to mutual feelings. The centrifugal force, working in and between women, is obviously present. If you look closely, however, it turns out that the personal aspect which makes everybody different is not sufficiently expressed ánd tolerated. There are female groups in which phase 3's ego-aspect is actually taboo. Former comrades from the feminist movement were very upset when Hedy d'Ancona, as a minister, made use of the official car with chauffeur, thus, according to them, falling for the ego-behaviour of a ministerial post. A 'real woman' should not present herself in a male way and should definitely not strive for a 'male' career. The 'should not' points to imposed norms and values and this is indeed the case. Within many feminist movement groups there are important unwritten laws for 'female behaviour'. These say: 'You may want and do what you like, as long as you remain nice and to everyone's taste. You may be ambitious, but you must not show it. However good you are, you must always say you cannot help it. You may climb higher, as long as the atmosphere remains pleasant. Show your insecurity and fears.[32] Hard work is all right, so long as you do not overdo it.' To complete the confusion, you are often told to remain yourself whatever happens.

This shows how, by self-imposed values and contradictions, women confuse each other and pull each other down. On the one hand, they signal that it is good to submit to the needs of phase 3. But at the same time, they point out that these must be implemented and brought into practice in the sense of phase 2. The norms in phase 2 say: 'Women (i.e., this category, group) behave in such and such a way. You must not act differently on your own; otherwise you will be struck from the group.' This means that your significance as a 'real' woman, in a group where these rules apply, is determined by the way in which you manage to comply with them. It is clear that if you, as a woman, are still very dependent on your surroundings, you will not easily be able to solve this problem.

Conquering the ego in male groups

Obviously, there are completely different problems regarding the ego in male groups from those in female ones. The Canadian trainer and consultant, Michael Kaufman, calls on men in lectures and workshops to emancipate and be a complete person at last. He sketches the development of a man as follows:

> From the age of about two, boys look around them and see: one day I will be powerful, one day everything will be mine. They learn to keep their emotions under control and they see that they must work, work, work in order to become a real man. But inside, they are still afraid and vulnerable. The result is that a life-long doubt nestles in them: *Do I make the masculine grade?* Am I enough of a man: am I successful enough, do I earn enough, am I good enough in bed?'[33]

This doubt leads to men's doing even more, working even harder, winning the hearts of women or using violence and aggression to prove that they really are tough and manly.

They want to show themselves and other men that they 'belong', that they are part of the male group. They confirm and strengthen the identity of the male group with this specific, traditionally male behaviour. As with the women, the men try to hold each other to these norms. If you are too 'soft', you do not belong. Having therapy is suspect too; it means you are weak. After all, a real man needs no therapy. That is only for women. 'We were afraid you would become a therapist freak,' a colleague once said to a man in his phase 4 crisis. He was a member of a group of advisers who were a group very much in the sphere of phase 3.

'The more afraid we are that we are not masculine enough,' says Michael Kaufman, 'the further away we get from our feelings and our humanity.' He points out that many men feel obliged to change because of their wife's emancipation. Through their own ego-development, women are no longer prepared to live entirely 'for the service of' and this leads to tensions in the relationship. If men wish to live properly with women, they must now make a move. Kaufman: 'We have our backs against the wall.'

This shows that in the man's soul, too, there is a fierce battle going on about his identity as a man and as a human being. On the one hand, there is the demand to be masculine according to traditional criteria and rules which have applied up till now. On the other, there are forces at work which pull in another direction, such as the ego-development and emancipation of women, and, of course (but this is usually not yet recognized) the urge for further development of the spirit in the phases 4, 5 and 6. This is a step which is impossible without contact with your own emotions, feelings and needs. The first impulse for change in the man comes from the outside, for instance the female emancipation, the second from the inside: the spirit Self.

Male groups where emotions and feelings are permitted and which are led by men are therefore very important for empowering further steps. Kaufman: 'The problem is that hardly anyone dares to be the first to speak, since the image of masculinity which they have internalized is so persistent. Only when one of us says he is vulnerable or frightened or unhappy do others think: oh, so I am allowed to feel that too.' This gives men, from soccer players to executives, a tremendous feeling of relief. Again we see how groups can hinder the growth of their members if they have little or no awareness about what human development is about. If, however, one or two dare to speak out, the others eventually have the courage to be themselves and this can, in the end, lead to a reversal of culture in the male group and from there to a different approach to masculinity.

The difference between yourself and your Self as a man

I must, however, make it clear that showing your feelings and emotions does not mean that you, as a man, have become your Self, that you have made contact with your inner core. This is often believed but it is a misconception. Feeling and undergoing your own subjective emotions and feelings still belong to the ego-stage — self with a small s. In the first instance, you feel what an occurrence, thought or other person does to *you*. You do not yet hear what the occurrence, thought or other person has to say. That only happens later, when you put your own experiences, which come from your ego, aside, free yourself inwardly and *really* listen from another layer, namely, that of your spiritual Self.

The challenge for the man to connect with feelings and emotions is at the same level as that of the woman to develop her own ego. It is the first step from the one-sidedness of one's own sex to a more whole person and thus to contact with one's deeper, spiritual Self. You become more whole by developing the dormant qualities (those which are prominent in the other sex) in yourself. You must, however, *integrate them in your already existing qualities and achievements*. Otherwise a man becomes a caricature of a woman and the woman a copy of the man. You learn to link them by trying, just as in phases 4, 5 and 6, to observe, feel and learn to understand, not only your own, but also the thoughts, feelings, needs and behaviour of other people.

Relationships between men and women

With regard to the different development through the phases of men and women, we can see a special problem in their relationship. Imagine the complicated situation if, for instance, the man is immersed in his emotions and sensitivities as a result of his inner crisis in phase 4 and his female partner is working on the gaps in her ego-development in phase 3. In that situation the man wants a warm, sympathetic woman to be there for him. But what if his partner has just chosen for herself to develop her more intellectual or male side through study or a responsible job? I have also come across women who hate the 'sentimental' man (in phase 4) their partner has become. They ask: where is the strong, intellectual man who can show me the way in the world, now that I need it for my ego-development? She cannot go to her male partner who is in phase 4. He has just left that 'ego and intellectual business' of phase 3 behind him and would hate it if his female partner were to land in it. Isn't she a woman? Well then, she mustn't try to be a man!

This shows how confusing it is nowadays, as people develop more strongly personally and, more than they used to, come to live in different phases. It also makes it clear that people lay claims on each other for their own development and think only of themselves in their expectations towards the other: 'She must be a loving, warm woman who is always there for me.' If that is not the case, they reproach each other. 'Where is the strong man who supports me in my conquest of the world?' If you do not understand this process and do not learn to handle it, you cannot progress, either alone or together, and you constantly come to a dead end in your private and working life. You also corner each other all the time. Again, reflection is the only solution: recognizing and putting into words where you both are and remaining open for the needs of the moment. You learn to deal with that by giving the other all the help and space they need. Luckily, there are couples who recognize this process and together find ways of giving shape to these complicated situations. An example.

The new community

A man is going through a personal crisis (phase 4), is working on himself, allows himself to have emotions and feelings and gradually becomes interested in spirituality. His partner has landed in phase 3, via her process in phase 4. She has taken on a responsible job and is presenting herself to the world. She wants to have nothing to do with spirituality. She is just trying to escape from the strict religious beliefs that were forced on her as a child. Each gives the other space for their own process but remains interested in the other's development. They are well able to talk about it. This, however, has not been achieved without difficulty and effort. In order to attain the strength and inner freedom they now both have, they have had to go through a crisis in their relationship. At first, the man found it difficult not to be able to share intimate issues with her, such as spiritual questions and insights for instance. He noticed too that she had become cooler and more distant. Insight into her process, however, made it clear to him that he had to accept her as and where she is and that he could not expect her to be as enthusiastic about new spiritual insights as he is. So he has learnt to curb this unfulfilled ego-desire.

In turn, she has learnt to listen to him with love and attention, to empathize but not to lose herself in the contact with him and, in particular, not to relate everything he talks about to herself. She tells him what she has seen and heard but does not feel responsible for the solution of his problems nor the need to 'talk him out of ' anything. She knows he can lead and change his own life. The only thing she can do to help him is to empathize and talk with him in a way that leaves him free. The man does the same to her.

What they are doing, in fact, is looking at the other's question or struggle from the other's point of view and empathizing. At the same time, they differentiate themselves from the other by not telling them how they themselves would deal with things. In this way they do not impinge on each other's territory or force the other to do anything. This shows that there are two important conditions to be fulfilled for this new approach: empathy and differentiation (empathizing but letting differences remain in existence). Empathy and differentiation are *the* two components for mature interdependence and involvement. One cannot live without the other. Men cannot do without female qualities, nor women without male ones. Just as men need women for their further development and women men. Only together do they become real human beings.

The man and woman described above are on their way to the new community, but not without regular setbacks that force them to work on their relationship again. They can only attain phase 6 if, each in their own way and at their own speed, and together, they continue to develop through the various phases—not forgetting to fetch time and again the bits of development that are left behind in earlier phases.

9. The Reflection Process

The need for reflection

In the previous chapters, the need for, and the necessity of reflection has often been mentioned. It is now time to give some attention to the reflection process itself. What is reflection? Reflection means: mirroring, considering, contemplating. It points to an activity: recalling something that happened, experiencing and considering it anew and discovering its meaning. You can reflect on something from the past, but also on current events and possibilities for the future.

The need for reflection is felt when we start questioning ourselves. You want to become aware of things: 'What is going on?' and to make conscious choices: 'How can I deal with it?'

The desire for contemplation begins in phase 4 and continues more strongly in phases 5, 6 and 7, the stages that lead to the increasing development of awareness. Of course, you also think about things in phases 2 and 3 – 'I see this or that happening' – and can alter course accordingly – 'so I must change this or that' – but this does not go as deep as the reflection in phase 4. There, the need for deeper insight, the meaning and significance, is felt. In phase 3, you are living in the layer of the ego, the outside of things. In phase 4 and after, you go to the layer of the spirit, the essence, the deeper knowledge and understanding, the truth – the inner side, in fact.

In earlier chapters we saw that, in phase 4, people on their individual life's road ask questions such as: How has my life been up to now? How did I feel about this or that? What have I omitted? What do I still want to do? They then use these questions to look at parts of their life, re-live and consider them again and thus find answers. By doing so they discover and come to understand the meaning and significance of their own life. The fact that we humans can reflect, question ourselves, and do something with the outcome is due to our being able to distance ourselves from the surroundings and from ourselves. The realization that you do not have to drown in your experiences, thoughts and emotions but can take distance from them is for many people a tremendous and rousing one. To illustrate this, I repeat what Ben Verbong, whom I cited in chapter 1, said: 'I awoke when I discovered that I could stand above things, not only in them. When I began to direct plays, I also got the feeling that I could largely direct my own life. The feeling that you can gain control, that you can steer things to a great extent and not just be steered.'

The road to freedom

Being able to take our distance and reflect means that we can think about ourselves and develop. In this way, we can get to know and change our old reaction patterns. We become aware: I am not only my moods, emotions or habits. Neither am I only what I happen to think and find at the moment. As a human being, I am not entirely dependent on my surroundings, other people or my moods and needs. I can take my distance from all that and determine my relationship to it. That makes me free and as a free person I can stand *in* myself, aware of my own strength. I can determine my own values and principles and live by them. I can develop my own talents and qualities. I can become pro-active instead of reactive, as the nurse in chapter 7 did. She became aware that she could choose for herself how to deal with her moody manager. Here too, we find that feeling of awakening, of freedom: 'I had the feeling I had been sentenced to death and had suddenly been set free. I wanted to shout as hard as possible: I am free! I will not let myself be governed by the moods of one man.' By reflecting on her behaviour and inwardly taking steps, the nurse opened the way to freedom in herself.

Capacity for reflection

How can we take the road towards self-knowledge and freedom? As a human being, you have a number of basic qualities.[34] These are:

- self-awareness
- imagination
- conscience
- free will
- feeling of responsibility

Self-awareness means that you can become aware of yourself, your situation and your Self, or, in other words, of yourself as an 'ordinary' personality, of your present position and of yourself as spiritual core. You can therefore gain insight and change.

Your *imagination* gives you the means to observe the situations you are in and, with the help of your capacity to think, form conceptions and impressions of them. This means you can form a picture of the past and the present and imagine where you want your life to go and how to make that happen.

Your *conscience* enables you to become aware, to *feel* what is right and what is wrong, what is true and what is false, what is just and what unjust. Through your feelings, your conscience opens the way to the fundamental principles and values living deep inside you which are essential to your life-vision. Your conscience helps you develop according to these moral standards. Thanks to it, you are able to check whether your thoughts, feelings and behaviour correspond to those principles and values.

You also have *free will*. This enables you, on the basis of self-awareness, imagination and conscience, consciously to choose how you deal with things in and around you, independently of whomever or whatever else.

Together, these capacities enable you to *take responsibility yourself* for your own situation, your thoughts, behaviour and feelings in the past, the present and the future.

Differences between people, animals and computers

The capacities mentioned above make us humans different from animals and computers. You cannot make any computer responsible for its 'deeds', its program. After all, it cannot change itself. It is not aware of itself. Everything it does is programmed and every program can be traced back to the actions of a person, the programmer. Animals, too, cannot reflect or act or change according to their insights. They have very limited possibilities, which are entirely governed by their bodily needs and instincts and their desires and discomforts.

Thus computers and animals know no freedom or

development on the basis of their own spiritual activity. They have no awareness in the shape of a personal spirit and no instrument in which this could work—an 'I' or personality. Therefore they have no self-awareness, no imagination and no freedom of choice. They have no conscience, no free will and therefore do not have a feeling of responsibility as humans do. As an 'I', I have a free spirit and a personality, I can stand in myself, take distance from myself and my surroundings, learn to know them and deal with them consciously. I can therefore change and develop and contribute to the development of my surroundings and of the world.

In principle, this development is unending because my spirit has an endless potential of forces for creative awareness, which will some day come to full fruition in me.

The reflection process

Thanks to our spiritual core, we are able to reflect. At the same time, this is a precondition for further spiritual growth. Since it is an awareness activity, we can only master this ability and learn how to handle it by trial and error. Reflection is, in fact, a process that has five different steps. What are they?

1. the current situation and the resulting questions, thoughts, feelings and needs;
2. analysis of the situation and the thoughts, feelings and needs;
3. deeper insight;
4. decision-making;
5. putting things into practice.

I have made a model for these five steps (see page 122).

I will describe them one by one, using Stephan Peijnenburg's story to clarify and comment on them.

1. *The current situation and the resulting questions, thoughts, feelings and needs*

In step 1, the situation in question is described, using the raised questions, emotions, feelings, thoughts, opinions, wishes, needs, etc. That of Stephan Peijnenburg can be described as follows. He works in his family's business: Koninklijke Peijnenburg Koekfabrieken in Geldrop. After 17 pleasant years, he becomes unsettled and asks himself the following questions: Is this all? Do I want to spend another 15 years making and selling honey-cake? Or is there something else? With these thoughts and questions about the current situation and a possible new one, his reflection process begins.

2. *Analysis of the situation and the thoughts, feelings and needs*

In step 2 you review the situation and the questions by collecting information and thinking about it, then arranging and analysing it. You can then come to a provisional conclusion. Peijnenburg, too, reviews the questions and the resulting feelings and wishes they bring up: Do I want to stay where I am or must I leave and go and do something else? He talks it over with the family and analyses the possible consequences: What will happen to the family business?

He comes to the conclusion that he needs more time. He needs half a year to clarify exactly what he wants to do. Peijnenburg: 'If you go on working, you cannot get down to reflecting.' Together with his family, he looks at what is possible and what not and whether his ideas are backed up

The reflection model

1.
Situation in practice

Events, experiences in daily life and the perceptions, thoughts,
emotions, ideas, wishes, longings, etc. belonging to them
Observing

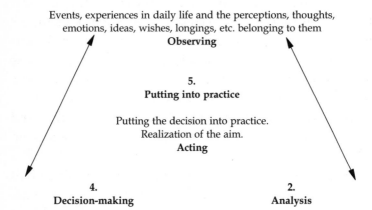

5.
Putting into practice

Putting the decision into practice.
Realization of the aim.
Acting

4.
Decision-making

Deciding.
How can I reach my goal?
What conditions need to be fulfilled?
What means are needed?
Action plan.
Willing

2.
Analysis

Gathering information.
Naming things, thinking.
Clarifying, sorting.
Thinking

3.
Deeper insight
Turning inward. Gaining insight, finding truth: idea, intuition.
Discovering the essence, feeling: This is it. This is true!
Understanding the deeper meaning, knowing.
Meaning and significance become clear.
What do I want to do with this?
What are the possibilities?
Feeling

by them. The availability of a good interim director is the deciding factor and he goes on leave for half a year.

3. *Deeper insight*

In the first place in step 3, you gain insight into the actual state of things. You see the inner connections and discover the truth behind them. Secondly, on the basis of this, it becomes clear what you want to do about them. In this layer you always, consciously or unconsciously, come across values and principles that are fundamental for you. Step 3 begins when you regularly take distance from your daily round, turn inward to look for insight and truth and for pointers which help you make the right choices, in other words, when you start to consider, to reflect.

To gain the necessary depth, you take the questions and considerations to heart, experience them, feel them, think them over, put the insights you get into words and then relinquish them again. After some time, you look at your questions and considerations again through your feelings and repeat the process. This picking up and letting go again is needed in order to attain the necessary depth. If you do not do this, you will never find the essence and will get stuck in step 2. Meanwhile, it can be useful to look into all sorts of practical questions relating to your search. This inner reflection (feeling – thinking – feeling, etc.) is repeated until things become clear. An answer can then appear in a sudden brainwave, a flash of insight: Now I know: this is it! This is what it is all about! Sometimes the road ahead is also shown: This is what I must do! But the answer can also come gradually and appear in all sorts of ways, for instance in a dream or during a walk when you are not thinking of anything in particular, or in a song that keeps running through your head.

A woman who was reflecting in this way about moving to another city, and wondered whether the time was ripe, suddenly heard a Beatles' song in her head: 'Wait'. The refrain ran through her head all day and she realized that the time for such a step was not yet ripe.[35]

By this inner activity, you are in fact submitting your questions and considerations to your higher Self in your innermost. This spiritual Self has a consciousness that is far greater and more inclusive than the thinking of your ordinary self. Through taking such a contemplative, meditative stance in which you are alternately inwardly active and then let everything go and rest, you make contact with this inner being. This now has the opportunity to give you the right answer or the deeper insight. An answer from the deeper layers of the soul can always be recognized immediately. You feel and know at once what the essence of something is: This is it!

Such a process takes time. Sometimes the answer comes quickly, sometimes it takes a little longer. Peijnenburg had his after a search lasting three months. He took the question 'Do I want to go on making and selling honey-cake for another 15 years or is there something else for me to do?' into himself, together with the idea that he wanted to make people think and his seeing that society was becoming increasingly egotistic. He also wanted to be an example to his children.

The first thing that becomes clear to him during his period of contemplation is that he does not want to return to the old business, the honey-cake factory in Geldrop, but to do something else. As soon as he is clear about that, all sorts of things happen. Peijnenburg: 'Things then come to you by themselves. The blockade you felt before is lifted.' This is the sign that contact has been made with the real and authentic Self. All sorts of things start to move. You are shown the right way and meet the right people who can help you on.

During his search, Peijnenburg comes across the Max Havelaar Foundation and knows: This is where I want to work. That is the next thing that becomes clear to him. He feels and knows: The post I will get there makes it possible for me to put those values and principles which are essential to me—pointing out to managers where their social responsibility lies and caring about a decent existence—into practice. That is where I can fulfil my mission.

4. Decision-making

In this step, what became clear in step 3 is consolidated in a decision: That is what I am going to do! That is where I must go! Then the next question is: What conditions must be met to make this possible? What is needed? How do I handle all this? In other words: What steps must I undertake to reach my goal?

Stephan Peijnenburg's story does not mention how this step went, but it is clear that much had to be arranged, since his leaving the business had all sorts of consequences. And undoubtedly there were many things to arrange for his new post with Max Havelaar.

5. Putting things into practice

At last the step is put into practice. What became clear in step 3 and was decided on in step 4 now begins, becomes reality. In Peijnenburg's case it meant that six months after he asked himself those fundamental questions he is working as Director of Marketing and Communication with Max Havelaar. He is successful. After a year, he says: 'Very gradually I see both the consumers' and the producers' awareness growing. Max Havelaar has a role to play in this and I can contribute to that.'

In his case, too, you can see the feeling of satisfaction, one could almost say fulfilment, which comes from contributing to the awareness and development of others and the greater whole by one's personal mission.

The increase of awareness and contact with the spirit

Many people who learn to use the reflection model in training sessions become aware of how superficial and unstructured their gaining of insight and decision-making usually is. Looking back at processes in which they have had to make decisions, it is often obvious that the original question in step 1 was not properly and clearly formulated. This, of course, influences the entire further process of awareness. Others realize that, although they analyse their question or problem in step 2, they immediately proceed to steps 4 and 5—deciding and immediately implementing the decision. Step 3 is then omitted and the decision-making process is gone through very quickly. The result is that they did not have contact with the deeper layer in themselves and thus not with their fundamental values and principles which should be the supporting motive for their decisions and actions.

By using all five steps of the reflection model in your search for the answers to your question, you draw on your entire soul and, with that, on your spiritual Self. Just as we use our body with hands and feet as an instrument for living, our spirit uses the forces of our soul—thinking, feeling, and will—as an instrument for awareness. In the reflection-model I have described, you use these soul-forces, together with observation and action, in purposeful combination. You will see that, in each of the five steps, one of these forces is emphasized. This does not mean that the others do not come into play in that step, they certainly do, but the main emphasis is on one particular force.

In step 1, the main thing is to observe the current situation and from there to formulate the right question. In step 2, analytical thought is central; in step 3, feeling; in step 4, the will; and in step 5, action in practice.

By using the reflection process in the right way, you appeal to the whole person and activate the higher, spiritual Self. Not only do you contact your own being, but also the deeper layers of life itself. In other words, through the reflection process, what we discussed in phase 4 of the individual road of the phase-mode is realized. This is finding the essence of and connection to the world of the spirit, the active awareness.

Using the reflection model

I would like to point out that the reflection model is applicable to any question, any step you wish to take, and any thought, feeling or problem for which you do not have an immediate solution or for which you want to find an answer that comes from the core. These questions can be about yourself, your relationship with other people, your work, a technical problem, collaboration, etc. They can be about the past, the present or the future.

Use of the model can prove difficult at first. You must always overcome a certain resistance in your ego in dealing with questions and problems in such a conscious way. You must also really get to know and use the various stages. For instance, what is the difference between step 2 and step 3? Patience and practice makes perfect.

One of the things that become clear to you is the importance of formulating your original question or problem clearly. In order to do this well, you may often have to go through (part of) the reflection model several times. When the question or problem has become clear to you, you again go through the model, now in order to find the answer to your question. The test of whether you have really found the essentials in phase 3 is the feeling of reassurance and inner peace that you get. It is a feeling that generates inner certainty and stability and gives you the strength and energy to act. It is obvious that this process leads to a manifestation of something from the spiritual world in day-to-day reality, where it becomes active.

Reflection in the team

You can reflect individually or with others in a group or team. It is, however, important that, before reflecting with others, you contemplate the question or problem alone, using the reflection model. Only then can you go through the reflection process together.

The step towards reflecting in a group or team is too great for many people. This is because you have in fact to go through a double reflection process: in yourself and together. For many, this is too much at the same time. It is best to help each other individually—maybe in small groups—first to gain clarity with the help of the reflection model. Only then do you start on the collective process. This method increases the involvement and motivation of the team members, strengthens the collective decision and forms new bonds among those concerned.

PART THREE: ORGANIZATIONAL DEVELOPMENT

10. The Development Road of Commercial Organizations

Organizations also develop. As with individuals and groups, seven different phases can be discerned. In their essence, these phases are the same in content as those I described for the individual and social development road. They are, however, different in character and therefore have other names. To make this clear, I have put the phases of individual/social development next to those of organizations:

Individual development	Development in organizations
1. Undivided unity	1. The theocratic organization
2. The old group	2. The autocratic organization
3. The 'I'-person	3. The bureaucratic organization
4. The transformation	4. The transforming organization
5. The spiritual Self	5. The organization based on moral principles and values
6. The new community	6. The organization as new community
7. Differentiated unity	7. The organization as contributor to world development

Development processes in organizations are complicated. One is not dealing only with the organization as a whole, but also with the development processes of individual members and teams. In order to get some insight into this complex whole, we need to have a clear picture of the essentials of the various stages of development.

A general description of the different phases which commercial organizations go through is given below.

Phase 1: The theocratic organization

For a good picture of phase 1, we need to go far back in time, to ancient Egypt, some three thousand years BC. The ancient Egyptians believed the world was flat and that Egypt was the centre of the world. To people living in those days, everything could be related to a whole with a centre. This can be seen at phase 1 in the phase diagram on page 36. The priest-king or Pharaoh was that centre. He was in contact with the world of the gods and was at the same time the representative of the gods on earth and executor of their will. Heaven and earth, the immaterial and the material were joined in him. This position gave him power and an almost godly status. In ancient Egypt, all life was led according to godly guidelines and laws which were read from the stars. Society was theocratically structured and completely hierarchical. Everything—land, people and people's lives—belonged to the Pharaoh, God's deputy on earth. As priest-king, the Pharaoh was both the religious and the secular leader. An individual human consciousness did not exist at that time. People felt themselves part of a greater whole that encompassed the entire earth and was guided and inspired by the world of the gods.

Religious and secular leadership

After the hey-day of Egyptian culture, this combination of religious and secular leadership in one person disintegrates. Emperors and kings become the secular leaders, Popes and bishops the religious ones. For centuries they fought for power and leadership over people and humanity as a whole. At first, the religious leaders triumphed in the western world. Later, after the Middle

Ages, power gradually went to the secular leaders. In our day, secular leaders — governments and parliaments — dominate over the leaders of religious movements. In the western world, ecclesiastical and religious laws are sub-servient to those of the state. Even today, however, we still find remnants of ancient Egypt's theocratic orientation. They can be recognized in the state-leaders' striving for rule and supremacy over the world and the wish to impose their way of thinking and doing on others, and also in sects under an absolute leader who is almighty and pulls all the strings within his community. An example of an organization that still has many elements of theocratic culture is the Roman Catholic Church. The Pope is head of the Church and is both the secular leader (The Vatican is a state) and the religious leader. Within the Roman Catholic Church, he is seen to be God's representative on earth. He is responsible only to God for his deeds, not to the believers or his closest assistants.

Something of the former godly powers that surrounded royal leaders in the past can be found in the term 'King/Queen by the grace of God', in use up till this very day.

Phase 2: The autocratic organization

This hierarchic type of leadership was still to be found in the nineteenth and twentieth centuries in businesses everywhere. Only in our day is this gradually changing. This type of autocratic organization is usually found in a family business with a very hierarchical power-relation-ship between employer and employee, where equality in communication is out of the question. The boss or owner-director has the ideas and thinks about what and how things must be done. He makes the decisions and sees to it that the employees fulfil their tasks and orders. The style of leadership is authoritarian and paternalistic. The employees themselves are passive and obedient. Anything like taking initiatives or responsibility does not exist. They learnt the trade from the boss or their superiors by practical experience.

This type of autocratic organization was able to exist because people — employees — at the time were mostly in the development phase 2, 'the old group'. The business was run like a family group, providing warmth and security. The boss or superior had a paternal way of giving leadership to the business and the employees — often called labourers or workers. Besides being paternally good-natured, he could also moralize. His influence often impinged on the employees' private life as well. An example of the atmosphere in a paternally led nineteenth-century business can be found in the history of the former Nederlandse Gist- en Spiritusfabriek in Delft. Mr and Mrs Van Marken, founders of the factory, felt sorry for the situation their workers were in and, as the first in the Netherlands, introduced a sort of social policy. They built a garden-city for their labourers next to the factory. These as subordinates, however, had little freedom. For instance, the Van Markens decided there should be no 'best room' in the houses. The best room was loved by the workers' wives because there they could show off their Sunday china and their best furniture. The Van Markens thought this superfluous, so no best rooms were built in the houses.

Besides the workers' village, the Gist- en Spiritusfabriek was also the first in the Netherlands to have a sort of workers' council. The first council, founded by Van

Marken in 1878, consisted of 20 higher officials, nominated by him, and three elected workers. The idea was that they should exchange views on their interests at meetings, but the workers hardly dared to say anything in the presence of their superiors.[36]

Courses in leadership did not then exist. The person who led the business did so on the basis of his own intuition and knowledge handed down from father to son. The paternalistic leaders of the time had a natural authority and feeling for leadership. One could say that there was still something of the ancient powers in them that had inspired the priest-kings from the world of the gods.

Phase 3: The bureaucratic organization

After the Second World War, changes in business take place in rapid succession. Welfare increases and technology is developed, resulting in increased production and distribution. This calls for radical changes in the organization. Work is divided into tasks and duties. Organization and efficiency bureaux appear and, using all sorts of labour analyses, introduce a number of administrative systems. Bureaucracy enters the organization.

As can be seen from the phase model (page 36), a characteristic of phase 3 is the disintegration and independent continuation of various parts which, in phase 2, had still been connected. The disintegration process is apparent from the division of work into tasks and duties, in the growing independence of staff members and yet later in the division of organizations into separate autonomous departments and teams.

Management

In order to have the independent parts cooperate, systems and procedures are needed which in turn have to be managed. This has lead to the introduction of the manager and later to the management team. It is management's task to ensure that the complicated system of collaborating people and technologies runs smoothly. Its most important tasks are: planning, budgeting, organizing, employing people, checking and solving problems. At first, management is one person's task, the successor of the autocratic leader of phase 2. Later on, this task is increasingly placed lower down in the organization because the decentralized departments and sub-departments each get their own managers. At this stage, leading a business is no longer a question of intuition and natural leadership but of plain professional skills and expertise.

The introduction of the manager therefore resulted in a host of courses in management and in the related term, 'permanent education'. Continual developments in technology and management demand a continual process of learning and development in everyone. That is why phase 3 is often called the 'phase of professionalization'.

The 'I'-phase and the physical instrument

Phase 3 in organizations contains two important developments. The first can be compared to the 'I'-phase of the individual; the second forms the basis for the development of the physical instrument of the organization.

Externally, the 'I'-element is recognizable in the division of the work into different duties and tasks. Internally, the organization is characterized by a strong development of the 'I'-personality and ego-behaviour of the people working in the company. More of this later.

The physical instrument of the organization develops because it is given form and structure. Like a person who has a physical body with which to live and work on earth, the physical body of the company is made up of the systems and procedures that guide the work-processes. The operator of these processes is the manager. He fulfils the 'I'-function of the organization, in the same way as the human 'I' operates and guides the person's thoughts, feelings and behaviour.

A company must, of course, have a good physical instrument. Just as an infirm, weak or sick body influences a person's life, so can the structure of an organization create illnesses and prevent further development, while the right form can promote the desired development. Phase 3 is therefore a very important one.

Changes in the employee

While the developments in management described above are taking place in the years after the Second World War, the style of leadership is at first very hierarchic, based on authority and power which demand compliance. The chief is the boss and you have to do what he says, whether you agree or not. A certain number of tasks must be finished within a certain period of time and the worker must see to it that the desired production is met with. The company's need for productivity and quantifiable results is central; the employee is only important because of the work he does. His own needs do not count.

In the 60s and 70s of the twentieth century, however, changes in this attitude occur. The democratization movements start up in the trail of student protests. Employees demand participation and want to be involved in planning and decision-making. This development later leads to the recognition of participation, institutionalized in workers' councils or in representative advisory bodies in companies and government institutions by the law on participation. The democratization movement has been of great influence on the development of organizations and is the direct result of the awakening of people's personal ego-awareness.

Employees become aware of what they personally want. They have their own opinions and do no longer want to walk on a lead or be walked over. I have described this process of the 'I'-development at length in Part One, of this book (under Phase 3). The individual employee speaks up and is discovered. As a result, his position within the organization changes completely. Not only does he get the opportunity to participate, but he is also seen as a sort of investment capital. 'Human resources management' is developed. Training and courses are designed to let the employee function optimally. The competence grows, and so does his or her responsibility and authority.

The next step is that the leadership of the organizations becomes conscious of the fact that such independence in the job is only possible if the employee gets the opportunity to also develop his or her own personality (phase 3!) and, in parallel, their own feeling of self-esteem.

Inner change in the executive
Motivating employees in such a way that they use their specific capacities to the full towards the aims of the organization and achieve satisfactorily requires an entirely different style of leadership than the autocratic one. The executive must ask himself: How can I achieve such interaction with my co-workers that their contribution is as

effective as possible and advances the development of the organization?

This demands a different approach from the executive towards his employees. In the past the badly educated worker was usually seen as a stupid and lazy fellow who had to be watched and checked and all the time told what to do. Nowadays, the employee is someone who wants to develop, who wants to understand, make decisions and solve problems himself, and thus play an active role in the organization.

In management and leadership training the executive is shown that it is only possible to increase the effectiveness of the modern employee if you meet these needs and wishes and approach each one of them personally. For nowadays every employee wants to be paid attention to and understood and supported by his or her superior, personally as well as professionally and in their aspirations.This means that the executive must learn to empathize with the employee and come to know and understand his problems and needs, weaknesses and potential. Only then can he give real guidance. This requires the ability to empathize, to interact and advise and an approach aimed at collaboration and development. These qualities are summarized in the term *interactive leadership*. Instead of only giving orders and emphasizing production and result, the modern executive also approaches the employee as a human being in development. He explains, questions, listens, gives feedback and tries to solve problems jointly. He is available for help and advice and engenders security and trust through an open approach and interest. Not every executive is able to handle this new method easily, but he who attempts it gets a firm bond with his co-workers. Instead of a boss who supervises and gives orders, the executive now functions as a sort of guide, who coaches the employee towards ever-growing independence. But even in this phase, a hierarchic type of policy exists.

In phase 3, many executives allow their employees to join in discussions and ask their opinion on certain questions, but in the end it is they who make the decision: This is how we are going to do it!

Bureaucracy

Characteristic of a company in phase 3 is that everything is aimed at reaching goals and getting results. This focus is revealed by the fact that the approach and the discussions between the executive and the employees are nearly all targeted towards some useful end, such as, for instance, the prevention of absenteeism or the improvement of performance. Even the 'how-are-you' conversations are often used as management instruments. Results are all-important. Targets must be met. For this, management is constantly geared, with the help of new, advanced systems, techniques or skills, to improve planning or budgeting and to stimulate employees to do just that little bit more.

Everything is aimed at perfecting the system, making the work processes maximally manageable and controllable, both materially and financially, so that maximum output is achieved.

Division and competition

In particular, those who are going through the 'I'-phase in their personal development feel at home in the achievement atmosphere of the bureaucratic organization. To present yourself and compete with others in reaching the targets, the competition element, is a challenge that appeals to many people in phase 3. Because people are led by ego-motives, we see in organizations that behaviour patterns appear in which the employee places him/herself in opposition to others. They think and act in terms of me and you. This happens between managers and employees as well as between employees. Ego-stimulating behaviour is, for instance, seen when someone holds back information or ideas, criticizes indirectly, keeps quiet if their own position is endangered or says things the boss wants to hear. This is often done for personal gain.[37] Ego-behaviour is also found where executives play their employees off against each other, in order to spur them on to higher achievements.

In most companies in phase 3, in particular in the telecom sector, departments obtain an increasing amount of autonomy and are often encouraged to compete with each other to get the highest results. A department that regularly achieves too little risks reorganization.

In such surroundings, people react by shutting themselves off from others and only concentrate on themselves. This strengthens their own ego—the phase 3 phenomenon—thus making mutual communication and collaboration even more difficult. The result is an atmosphere of division, mistrust, negativity and despondency in the company. Employees feel left out, are thrown back on themselves and become indifferent—after all, there is nothing they can do about it! Very often these negative effects are then countered by new and improved checks and rewards systems.

It is clear that such a culture undermines the development of people and organizations and has no future.[38]

Consequences of phase 3

Today, most companies and organizations are in phase 3

and demonstrate its aspects, both positive and negative. The systems approach works well if it is subservient to the main task of the organization, but it has a negative effect if thinking in systems becomes an aim in itself and strengthens the one-sided tendencies of phase 3. Some examples show these clearly, together with their far-reaching consequences.

De Nederlands Spoorwegen (Dutch Railways)
The first is the Nederlandse Spoorwegen (NS). In 1992, politics decided that market forces and competition should be introduced into the railways. The NS became independent, privatized and split into different departments dealing with rails, signals, electricity supply and traffic control (cf. British Rail). Other parts became independent or were sold off. The company, which, from the workers' point of view still had the family feel of phase 2, was dragged into phase 3 in one fell swoop. The employees felt they had lost their 'home'.

As is usual in phase 3, each independent department developed its own vision and aims and thought only of its own interests. In the absence of a coordinating plan or central control, the 'I'-function was not fulfilled. The now independent departments did not cooperate, or not enough, and the main task — transport of people — was lost out. The greater whole was lost sight of. The results are well known. Not only customer satisfaction, but also the morale of the employees, once so proud of 'their railway', dropped to unprecedented depths. This was reinforced by the distance and lack of understanding between the top management and the employees in this bureaucratically led organization. The result was that absenteeism among the employees rose sky-high.

Social services
In the social services sector, expansion, by means of closure of small hospitals and home-care institutions and mergers with others, was promoted. Such mergers led to enormous social services institutions (cf the National Health Service), run on a commercial basis under leadership of a bureaucratic management, with supervision and control as its main activities. Expansion and commercial thinking also strengthened the tendency to turn care into a technique. Here too, the chasm between the managers at their desks and the care workers grew — and is still growing.

Managers, usually without a social services background, look mainly at the material and financial possibilities. The carers themselves, who once chose their profession in order to nurse and care for sick people, feel locked into a strict, technical system with a great deal of stress and lack of staff, which gives them little time or room to give patients the personal attention and care they need. The result is that carers leave the institutions *en masse* and here, too, there is huge absenteeism. This in turn results in departments of hospitals and nursing-homes having to close down and waiting lists getting longer.

Macho-managers
The biggest trap for executives of an organization in phase 3 is a certain addiction to their own ego and the status and power belonging to it. The chance that many (top) managers fall into it is great, especially since they are also in the ego-phase in their personal development and this is reinforced by their position in the company. Self-interest and retention of their own power and status effect all their decisions and — especially if there is little self-knowledge —

can even gain the upper hand, with all this entails for the organization.

An example of the excesses that appear when ego-aspirations and bureaucratic management meet and reinforce each other is the entrance of what is called 'macho-managers' in large companies.

These macho-managers only see one value in an enterprise: that of the shareholders. Their motto is reorganization, which they see as the only strategy for helping the company on. The Groningen professor Van Witteloostuijn, in his contribution to *Herpositionering van ondernemingen* (Repositioning of Companies), writes that this macho-management 'does exactly what it says it does not do, namely, destroy values instead of creating them'.[39] Van Witteloostuijn: 'The macho-manager tries, with the help of minimalization of costs, to achieve maximization of value. To this end, a broad scale of management concepts are brought into play, with the aim of producing ever more with ever fewer people (and thus lower costs). Enough is always too little and too much is never enough. Therefore "continual reorganization", by means of a never-ending succession of "improvement routes", is the everlasting motto of macho-management.'

Research between 1990 and 2000 in some 30 Dutch companies, however, showed that those who chose to reorganize their work-force eventually saw their profits fall. Research in the US points to the same conclusion. The reason for this, according to the professor, is that the continual reorganization gradually destroys the effective organization structures on which the company is based. The motivation of the remaining employees is undermined and decreases. Creativity on the shop floor is smothered. Talented members of staff leave the company and finally the learning potential of the company is harmed. In spite of this, the down-sizing, aiming to increase the profits and financial worth of the company, goes on. The stock exchange and shareholders are all-important and the wishes of all the others involved are subservient to this and of secondary importance.

In the light of the increased popularity of share-bonuses for top managers, we can see that they now primarily serve their own interests by focusing on the value-development of the company's shares.

Getting stuck in phase 3

The 'ego-atmosphere' of an organization is characterized by the emphasis on personal aspiration, position, mutual competition and assessment of achievement. This one-sidedness takes its toll, as we have seen. Mutual separation, mistrust and negativity make for an atmosphere in which there is little space for growth. Employees notice that they are thrown back on themselves and can find no solution, either personally or together. They feel stressed and empty and become apathetic and discouraged.

In the terms of this book, one could say that the employees unconsciously feel that the organization is shutting them up in their own phase 3, while deep inside they want to go further and are longing for the next phase, where things take on meaning and significance and the soul comes to life. The same is true of their relationship with each other. As we have seen earlier, people always want growth and progression. If this cannot be realized, disappointment and negativity set in, expressed by some in aggressive behaviour, by others in flight: depression, apathy or discouragement.

When, in spite of yet another reorganization and the

introduction of new management and control systems, growth stagnates, sales decline, customers are discontented and there is a high rate of absenteeism and people leaving, the organization may come to the conclusion that it is stuck, just like the employees who find they are not getting any further.

Experts point to the fact that decline can be due to external factors, such as developments in technology, market movement or competition, but that, more often than is thought, there is another reason. That is the organization's inward-looking tendency and the management's obstinate sticking to numbers of deeply entrenched patterns of thought and reaction.[40] The outdated approach is then to blame. A completely new way of thinking is needed, which leads to new steps being taken—new steps which break with the principle of 'more of the same' and in which things are devised and handled in a radically different way, in short, in which the organization moves on to phase 4.

Phase 4: The transforming organization

When does an organization reach phase 4? When, for whatever reason, the decision is made to relinquish the old orientation and take the real task of the organization as the orientation-point. The old orientation came from the outside, the new one comes from within. In phase 4, the step from outside to inside must be taken and the connection made to the real essentials. One could also say: the path to the spirit must be taken—the working fundamental, the active awareness principle of the organization. For, like an individual, a collaborating unit of people, as in an organization, has a soul with a spirit working within it, an active spiritual principle. Like a human being, the organization is a living organism, with its development laws, growing and wanting to unfold its being. That being, that spiritual principle, is expressed in the mission, the identity of the organization and the vision and values that it entails.

Mission and values

The mission is the reason for the company's existence. But it is also a directive: Why are we here? What are we here for? What is our contribution to the greater whole?

Some will immediately say that a commercial company has only one mission—expanding and making as much money as possible. You can look at it in that way but that is an example of phase 3 thinking. You can also see it in a broader sense: every organization, by its existence, its services and its goods, contributes to the development of the greater whole—society. Whether your company makes gas-pipes or food, both are needed for the continuation and further development of society. The only question is: What is your motive in doing so? Does your organization work solely for its own (continued) existence, attempting to gain as much profit as possible meanwhile, or do you have (an)other motive(s)? For instance: I want to produce my foodstuffs in such a way that they contribute to people's health and welfare. In other words, I want to do things in such a way that not only I profit from them but I can also contribute positively to the community. You see that your company has its place in society because it derives its justification from it and gives something in return. Its justification is that it produces food for the community. Its added value, in the sense of phase 4, is that you do that consciously, from certain motives or values: so that the health and welfare of the greater whole, the community, is improved.

In phase 4, your mission is based on deeper-lying values, on what you find important for other people, society, the world, the earth, such as 'open communication with the customer', 'every employee in our company must be able to develop himself', 'in seven years all our products must be recyclable', and so on. These values, together with the mission, form the spiritual element of the organization. They do not come from outside, nor from the ego, but from the spiritual core inside and are related to the basic tasks of the company. Values, mission and vision determine the identity and individuality of the organization.

Identity and vision

Values answer the question: What do we, as organization, think important? What do we represent? Identity shows who you are as an organization: Who are we? A good mission statement summarizes all that. It shows who you are (identity), what you represent (value) and what your unique contribution as an organization is (mission). Southwest Airlines, a very successful airline company in the United States, summarizes its mission as follows:

> The mission of Southwest Airlines is dedicated to the highest quality of customer service delivered with a sense of warmth, friendliness, individual pride, and company spirit ... We are committed to provide our employees a stable work environment with equal opportunity for learning and personal growth. Creativity and innovation are encouraged for improving the effectiveness of Southwest Airlines.[41]

This statement shows who they are and what their values are. These express the involvement of Southwest Airlines with their customers and employees and their caring approach to them.

The vision of a company shows where the organization, with its values and mission, is heading. Suikerfabriek (Sweets factory) Van Melle, one of the first Dutch companies to base its business on values, says of the fundamental values of the company:

Giving priority to principles which are of primary importance to people's lives and to nature – in short, to creation – now and in the future.

Their vision is:

This includes a proposal for radical change. All ecologically irresponsible activities will be altered so that in 20 years' time these will all be sustainable and we are gradually restored to harmony with our natural surroundings.[42]

The vision can be about the product that is made, but also about the organization itself, such as aspiring to personal leadership and the social responsibility of the employees. The contribution made to the development of the world or to creation can also play a part.

The transformation process

The transformation process of an organization, whether it is a company or an institution, must connect to its core, from there defining the entire organization anew and reforming it in all its facets. It begins with a very careful definition of the values and mission of the organization. The way in which these can be expressed throughout the organization must be laid down in action-plans: in the production and work-processes, in the materials used, in the way in which customers and staff are treated, in decision-making, labour conditions, personnel care and public relations, and then put into practice.

This cannot be done just like that. It necessitates many years of intensive effort, involving everybody in the organization, from high to low. Such a turn-about in the culture demands very radical changes in awareness and action.

A transformation process like this can only succeed if it takes place in the inner self of all the employees and in all the layers of the organization. As Van Melle says, we must count on its taking at least some ten years, just as it does in the transformation process in a person's life.

Clearing up the past

Transformation necessarily also opens up the organization's past. Discussions about the values and principles that will govern the procedures of the organization in the future automatically illuminate the values, deals and solutions that have governed life up till then. We cannot avoid first looking back. That is not easy. Many values are seen as normal and have implicitly become part of the company culture, but they are not easy to put into words because they live in the unconscious. Some things are simply not talked about—the taboos in the organization. It is, however, necessary to become aware of them and discuss them, otherwise they can counteract the new values.

Unspoken rules which determine the culture are, for instance: 'Here we obey orders', 'Always keep on the right side of the boss', 'Take no risks', 'Don't make mistakes', 'It's the results that count, not the people'. An organization in transformation must, like an individual, dare to admit what happened in the past and discover why. What is our history? What happened? How far are people involved? What needs to be brought into the open? What needs to be recognized and understood by others? What fixed ideas or suppositions are there? What values have governed our lives up to now? What must we keep? What must we change? What mistakes have been admitted? Has forgiveness been asked? Only after attention has been given to these questions can one look for what needs to be done. In my work as advisor to organizations, I have several times seen that the space necessary for taking new steps could only be found in the organization when the leadership or the managers admitted their mistakes or faulty suppositions and called in the help of others to avoid repeating them. This often occurred in meetings where you could hear a pin drop. These are very important moments which bring about a great deal. It is like breaking a spell. Only when such delicate things can be discussed does relaxation set in and trust gradually arise. And only then can you, as organization, look towards the future.

Marike van Lier Lels experienced this when she became director of Van Gend en Loos (a large Dutch transport firm). When she came, she found a company in a downward spiral with little mutual trust and bad communication. She, too, had to go back to the past and clear up old sores. That opened the road to the future: 'Now that there is mutual trust, I want to work on the strategy, talk about our vision. With the drivers as well.'[43]

From focus on results to focus on people
From phase 3 to phase 4 is a very big step, one in which the focus on achievement and results is relinquished and replaced by thinking based on values and people. For that

is what happens. Values can only be recognized and put into practice by people. This leads to *people being central* in the transforming organization and in the following phases 5, 6 and 7. They are central as individuals and as members of a team or department where individuals work together. The important thing is the person in the employee and the person in the excutive or manager. I will return to that later.

Does the transition from phase 3 to phase 4 mean that you can or may no longer make a profit? Of course not. But it does mean that the idealistic, non-material becomes just as important as the material, the making of profits. In phase 4, there is therefore a certain balance between material, ego-focused needs and immaterial, higher values, whereby the former never become more important than the latter.

Some companies in phases 4 and 5 even put their employees first, before their shareholders. A successful American menswear company, The Men's Wearhouse, with sales of eight-hundred million dollars, states that the concern has five groups of interested parties.[44] In order of importance, these are: the employees, the customers, the suppliers, the community and, finally, the shareholders. The firm assumes that there is a relationship between the loyalty of customers and that of employees towards the company. Employees who have a bond with the company will also build up a bond with their customers. Thus the vision of The Men's Wearhouse: 'We create a quality relationship with our people, and since we are in the retail business, hopefully they will create a quality relationship with the customer ... The best way to maximize share-holder value is to put that at the bottom of the hierarchy. By taking care of your employees, your customers, your vendors, and your communities, you will maximize long-term shareholder value.' That is evident!

Metanoia

It is clear from the above that the emphasis of an organization in phase 3 is on the past, while that in a company or institution in phase 4 is on the future. In phase 3 there are attempts to perfect the management and control-systems to such an extent that an ever better management—from outside—is made possible. However, there is really nothing new. All that is 'new' is, in fact, just more of the same. The status quo is all the time maintained. The developments in phase 3 are therefore doomed to fail in the end.

In organizations in phase 4 (and those in 5, 6 and 7), the managers have a vision of the future and work towards it. Their vision is based on a development process coming from the inner core, in universal values and principles, which—since they are spiritual—have an unending potential and make an entirely new form of management from the inside possible.

The transition from phase 3 to 4—as I already pointed out—demands a change of awareness which is not only apparent in the way of thinking, but also in a different inner attitude and approach.

Besides transformation, this turn-around in thought and action is sometimes called *metanoia*, a Greek word meaning 'fundamental change of thought and insight'. It was already used in bygone days to denote this process of inner change. In the Greek translation of the Bible, John the Baptist, who lived more than two thousand years ago in ancient Israel, uses the word metanoia when he warns people that the olden times are over and a new time has come, one that demands a completely different approach and way of thinking and acting.

About 25 years ago, innovative thinkers in the field of organization development, such as Peter Senge and Charles Kiefer, used the term 'metanoic organizations' to denote those companies making such inner changes.[45] The term metanoic organizations, however, did not catch on and is now hardly ever used, but it expresses exactly what takes place in phase 4.

Phase 5: The organization based on moral values and principles

It is only some 25 years since organizations in general started to develop characteristics belonging to phase 5. I use the phrase 'started to develop' purposely, since there are as yet no companies or institutions actually in phase 5. What are these characteristics? Organizations based on moral values and principles share five essential aspects:[46]

1. They have strong aims, expressed in a mission and a vision based on moral values and principles. Through this, there is in the present an orientation-point which indicates future developments.
2. Mission and vision create enthusiasm and involvement among the employees and coordinate the work of very different individuals, while each has their own contribution.
3. Individuals are encouraged to achieve, to do their best to develop and grow personally, to display initiative and to feel as responsible as if they were co-owner of the company.

4. The structure of the organization, each individual role —
   responsibility, policy, information and so on — is
   designed to give maximum support to the realization of
   mission and vision. To this end, constant improvements
   and adjustments are made. Companies in phase 5
   usually have very decentralized powers of decision and
   responsibility, unusually flat hierarchies and little
   bureaucracy. Some have even broken altogether with
   the traditional hierarchic structure.
5. Besides reason and rational analysis, importance is laid
   on feeling, inspiration and spiritual insight. By this is
   meant the process of awareness described in the
   reflection process on page 122 in chapter 9. Through
   their own personal growth in phases 4 and 5, executives
   and employees empower a unique interchange between
   the intellect and their feelings and thus attain deeper
   insight and spiritual inspiration.

Values and principles
How do companies in phase 5 put their values and principles into words and how do these have effect inside and
outside the organization? An example can be seen in the
American company, AES Corporation (originally Applied
Energy Services). AES is a radically decentralized company which owns more than a hundred power-plants and
distribution centres in 16 countries around the world. Each
location, from Kazakhstan to Argentina and Pakistan is run
by a team. The company has more than ten thousand
employees, and functions with a head office with less than
30 employees. From its foundation in 1981, emphasis is laid
on four core values and principles: integrity, honesty,
social responsibility and pleasure. These are defined by
AES as follows:

Integrity ... Integrity comes from the Latin word *integra*, which means 'wholeness'. By carefully weighing all factors ... AES strives to act with integrity in all of its activities.

Fairness ... [T]he term 'fairness' means 'justice'. Often 'fairness' is confused with 'sameness' ... We don't mean that. AES aspires to give everyone special treatment.

Social responsibility. The most socially responsible thing a corporation can do is to do a superb job of meeting a need in society. Therefore, companies must carefully manage capital, employees and intellect to meet a societal need. For AES, the first step ... is to ensure that every generating plant is operated in a clean, reliable, safe and cost-effective manner. But we have chosen to go beyond the essentials ... That is why we plant millions of trees to offset carbon dioxide and build new schools and take ... other steps to improve our environment and build communities.

Fun ... For us, 'fun' means establishing an environment in which people can use their gifts and skills to make a difference in society without fear of being squelched.[47]

Pleasure means that AES let their employees do interesting work and make their own decisions, face their own challenges and have the opportunity to learn and try things out.

Alignment and consistency

It is all very well to formulate beautiful values and principles, but the main thing is how to bring these into practice. Organizations in phase 5 agree. They therefore choose two important points of departure: alignment and consistency. To begin with, values and principles are continually under discussion and are set as an example by the (top) managers and other executives. Further, the organization attempts to express its values and principles in the entire structure of the organization, inside and out, and to attune them to each other and implement them consistently. This includes working and production processes, the attitude of executives and employees, the contact with customers and suppliers, the selection of personnel and public relations. Management practice must constantly support and confirm the values and principles. Without this, of course, everything is doomed to failure. A company with values and principles in its mission that does not live up to them in practice undermines its credibility, both inside and outside the company. For the employees, this is not only a sign that no one takes the values and principles seriously, it is also counterproductive. Instead of honesty there is dishonesty and falsehood in the company and this leads to disappointment and cynicism. Consistency in the attuning of values and principles in the organization is no easy task— it is, in fact, very difficult. It demands of management and employees continual alertness and awareness, imagination and adjustment.

Point of orientation
As you can see, values and principles are used as inner points of orientation for thinking, feeling and acting, both now and in the future. In this way, they help the organization to stay on course. A company in phase 5, faced with the question of whether or not to introduce a new policy, will first consider carefully whether this conforms (or could be made to conform) to the current values and principles. Only if this is so will further development and

implementation take place. The same attitude is to be seen regarding profit-making.

Dennis Bakke, the Chief Executive Officer (CEO) of AES, once said about making profits: 'Profits are to an organization what breath is to life. Breathing is not the aim of life, but without it life ceases. In the same way, a company that does not make profits ceases to exist.'[48] Maximizing profits, however, is not a prime aim of this company. They say:

> An important element of AES is its commitment to four major 'shared' values ... [I]f the Company perceives a conflict between these values and profits, it will try to adhere to its values — even though doing so might result in diminished profits or forgone opportunities. Morover, the Company seeks to adhere to these values not as means to achieve economic success, but because adherence is a worthwhile goal in and of itself.[49]

The American Security and Exchange Commission, which monitors security on the Stock Exchange, feels that this is such a threat to the Stock Exchange that it has ordered AES to mention their values as possible risk factors when bringing out new shares!

Values and principles provide executives and employees with a point of reference by which plans and decisions can be personally tested. This means that everyone is free to determine what they should do, with the result that everyone attunes to the core, thus retaining their connection to the essential — spiritual — principles of the organization.

Employees

Employees of an organization have a deep desire to develop, not only their own ego, but also their own spiritual principles, the core of their being. In previous chapters, we saw that this is expressed in the desire and the capacity to take distance from oneself, to think about oneself and life in general and to get to know and use one's own values, principles and qualities. They also want to be at the helm, be pro-active, take initiatives, have responsibility and authority and contribute in a meaningful way.

Motivation

If one looks at what motivates employees nowadays to do their best, it is interesting to see that they do not, in the first instance, mention the work they want to do but the conditions which make the above possible.

John Whitmore discovered that there are three elements which can arouse enthusiasm in employees: the chance to take real responsibility and have freedom of choice, the chance to build up self-respect and a personal identity, and the chance to experience the feeling of really contributing.[50]

Other investigations mention that employees prefer companies where there is room for personal development and where there is good leadership and pleasant colleagues. Money appears not to be of most crucial importance, unless the salary is significantly below the market norm. If policy is right on the above points, employees will even take greater pressure of work in their stride.[51]

This shows how strong the incentive is in people today to develop both personally and spiritually in the way described above. This motive force is the greatest desire driving people on earth. It is *the desire for personal development in order to contribute, in collaboration with others, to the development of the greater whole.* One could say: 'That is what we are here for. That is the deeper reason for our wish to develop in this way. That is also why we want to develop personally in our work and have good colleagues with whom we can collaborate and work on the development of the greater whole.' At first, this may be one's own department, later the entire organization and eventually society. The more the aims of the organization correspond to the deeper needs and aims of the employees, the more enthusiastic and inspired they will be in their work.

Supporting such a process calls for good leadership.

What do organizations in phase 5 have to offer?
An organization in phase 5 differs from one in phase 3 in that it does not attach importance only to the achievements of the employees, their production. These organizations rouse their employees by appealing to their entire humanity and their possibilities for development. Some put this into words in their core values and company philosophy. The successful company Analog Devices Inc. (ADI), of Norwood, Massachusetts in the USA, which produces apparatus for automated measuring and control-systems, says:

> We believe that people are honest and trustworthy and want to be treated with dignity and respect.
> They want to realize their potential and are willing to work hard for it.
> They want to know what they are doing and what the aims are of the organization they are working for.
> They want to have influence on decisions on what is going to be done and how that is to be done.

They want to be responsible for the results and be appreciated and remunerated for their achievements.[52]

AES Corporation accentuates the humanity of their employees by careful use of wording. The term 'human resources' is avoided where possible. CEO Bakke: 'Steel is a raw material, people are not.' The word 'efficiency' is also used as little as possible. 'Efficiency is a technical concept, the relationship between output and input. It puts people on a line with machines.' And they are not machines.

The idea at the bottom of AES's thinking is that its employees are:

creative, thinking individuals ... [who] are responsible [,] ... desire to make positive contributions to society, associate with a winner and a cause, like a challenge [,] ... are unique persons, deserving respect, not numbers or machines.[53]

Attention and appreciation for the individual and their possibilities is translated by both ADI and AES into decentralized structure and dispersed decision-making. Power of decision is placed very low down in the organization. 'The essence of human beings, who we are as people, is our ability to analyse and make decisions,' says Bakke, '[I]f you don't have that, you can't even experience full humanness.'[54] The people at AES have therefore been given the power and responsibility for taking important decisions and behaving as though they were co-owners of the company and not just cogs in a machine.

The belief and trust in people that is so characteristic of organizations in phase 5 has resulted in AES being an organization of really self-managing teams, in which people do their own work and not only feel responsible for it but also for the welfare of the other members of the team and for the whole. They support each other because they realize that they are all not only part of the same whole, but also work together to develop that whole further.

Interaction between organization and employees

What does an employee notice about the difference between a company that only appeals to your production results and one which, in the first place, recognizes and appreciates you as a developing person? The difference is very great! In the first case, a large part of you is not seen and, since it is not seen or recognized, it cannot exist or develop. Not to be acknowledged in one's inner being penetrates deeply into the employees and has a discouraging effect on their feelings of self-respect. In our time, when people are awakening spiritually and look for inner growth, there is a great need for recognition and stimulation.

In phase 5 organizations – and sometimes already those in phase 4 – this spiritual potential is drawn on. People see *reflected back to them the picture of who they really are, what their potential is and what they really want, deep inside* ... That confirms them in their humanity and in their spiritual development. What does this lead to? Inner strength, energy and the courage to take steps! But there is more.

The moral values and principles on which the phase 5 organization is based are not only named, but also disseminated and brought into practice within and outside the organization. At AES, for instance, they try to put into practice the honest image of man and the core values: integrity, honesty, social responsibility and fun. This is visible to the outside world in the way AES runs its generating plants, plants millions of trees to counteract the emission of carbon dioxide, cooperates towards the further improvement of the environment and builds new schools to help develop local communities in the various countries. All this appeals to the deeper, spiritual layers of the employees. After all, the values and principles expressed in integrity, honesty, social responsibility and the will to contribute positively to something different and greater than themselves lives in all of them and *is part of their own spiritual being that wants to develop.* Moral values and principles and the will to contribute to the development of others and a greater whole come from a spiritual force that is in all men, that supports and organizes development and is individualized in man in his spiritual Self.

If an employee or candidate hears and sees how the organization brings these fundamental intentions into practice, it awakens something hidden deep inside; something that emerges from very deep layers and suddenly becomes conscious. All at once they know: This is what I want too! This is what I want to contribute to! I want to be part of that!

In this way, the basic principles and aims of the phase 5 organization is aligned to what the employees inwardly want. That mutually stimulates, develops and strengthens. The employees work with dedication, inspiration and enthusiasm on the work itself, in collaboration with colleagues and for the aims and development of the organization. In turn, the organization awakens and supports the personal, professional and spiritual development of its employees.

The above does not mean that this seemingly perfect combination works just like that. In practice, it demands a great deal of effort and development. That is also the reason why there are as yet so few organizations fully in phase 5. In order to make the phase 5 process possible, a few of the (top) executives must already to some extent have developed spiritually, otherwise it will not work. And that takes time. Spiritual development always goes against the current, and results have to be secured time and again. Organizations that have already taken the first steps towards phase 5 will have to be continually aware and alert in order to make adjustments and further development possible.

Without this, the organization will irrevocably recede quickly to earlier stages of development.

Executives

In the fifth development phase of an organization, employees have their own responsibilities and powers. Their entrepreneurship is stimulated and they are often, together with others, part of an independent project group or a self-managing team. This development brings about many changes in the tasks and duties of the executive. In the organization's phase 3, he was primarily a 'manager', directing and supervising the employees and their work. In phases 4 and 5 his task changes radically. Instead of managing the daily operations, the executive must now concern himself with mission, vision and the general course, with the development of core qualities, values and principles of the organization and with the development of employees—in other words, with the spiritual element.

Five aspects of leadership

In the functions and tasks of the executive in phase 5, there are five important elements:

1. The first task is to put the mission, vision, values and the culture of the organization into words and — in consultation with the employees — develop and disseminate these further, so that they provide inspiration for the surroundings.
2. To set an example by implementing these values and principles in her/his own thinking, feeling and acting.
3. To see to it that there is alignment and consistency between the values, principles, strategy, systems, culture and core capacity of the department or company.
4. To give such support to the employees that they can develop professionally and personally to the core of their being, can live according to their own values and principles and from there devote themselves to the aims of the organization.
5. To see to it that the various processes are coordinated. Using the core qualities as a basis, he must combine everything into a collaborating whole so that the stated aims can be realized.

Vision, values and principles

In phase 5, the development of vision, values and principles is of great importance. Vision gives direction and the values and principles the road to accomplishment. The importance given to the development of vision, values and principles is demonstrated by the fact that, in companies in phase 5, the CEOs do nothing but concern themselves with the aspects already mentioned. Bakke, the CEO of AES, considers it as his task constantly to see to it that the values and principles — justice, integrity and social responsibility — get through to all sections and so form the basis of the organization.

The executives of the American company Cisco

constantly emphasize customers' interests, economy, teamwork and the need to avoid all technological dogmas. In fact, all the (top) executives of phase 5 organizations recognize that their primary mission is to develop vision and confirm the values and principles of the company.[55] That process is a never-ending one. There are always new problems that question the core qualities of the organization and need dealing with. Of course, the executives do all they can to express the values and principles in their own life and work.

Support of employees
In phase 5, the two streams of development in an organization — that of the individual employee and that of the organization — come together in a special way. In this phase, the core, the being of the organization, wants to be expressed, as is visible in the mission, vision, values and qualities of a company. A company can, however, only realize this with employees who, through their own development, are able and willing to do this. A company where all the employees and executives are in the ego-phase (3), cannot possibly develop in a phase 5 sense. It needs people, executives in the first instance, who are taking steps in their personal life towards phases 4 and 5. It is in the self-interest of a company wishing to become familiar with moral values and principles that its employees develop in that direction, both personally and socially.

On the other hand, the employees also want to grow. They want to develop their own spiritual Self and its qualities and they look for work in a place that offers them opportunities for personal development together with executives who can give them good guidance, inspire and awaken them. No wonder that companies nowadays look intensively for inspiring executives who have the necessary qualities for this. It is important that they are able to create an atmosphere of openness, sincerity and security so that this development can take place.

As coach or counsellor, they help the employees to know themselves through their work. They let them gain experience, ask questions and have them reflect on their actions in order to learn from them. They encourage employees to work together as a team and to solve problems amongst them by themselves. Finally, they help their colleagues to live creatively and with the inner strength of their own values, so that they can apply their qualities and newly discovered abilities to the work of the organization.

Servant leadership

Comparison between the phase 5 executive and the one in phase 3 shows how very different they are. In phase 3, the executive is solely in charge and the input of employees limited. In phase 5, this restrictive role of the executive makes way for a stimulating one, that of developing that which lives in the core of the organization and in the spirit of the employees. The executive who does this is 'serviceable', in the service of the development of others. Leadership in phase 5 becomes *servant leadership*.[56]

Such a step demands an enormous inner reversal in the executive. It means you must put aside your own ego, with all its needs and desires, and, through another strength in yourself, try to understand and help the other. This looks easier than it actually is in practice because, as an executive, you experience a great deal in a phase 3 sense. See what you feel in yourself if the other knows less or has less ability than you and you are talking all the time and telling the other what you think they should do.

Nowadays, employees want to be independent. They no longer want to hear from others what to do; they want to find out for themselves. They need their superior, of course, to teach them something they do not know or cannot do, but they would rather gain insight themselves as quickly as possible and make their own decisions about what to do. For this, they need someone who is open to them, asks questions and listens so that they can go through the inner reflection-process in the right way. Servant leadership demands your being there for the employee and his/her task, and in particular that you listen and understand in an open, attentive, free and interested way. If you do that, something happens in them. Thoughts and feelings get, as it were, substance and direction. Suddenly they have a flash of insight and know what the next step must be.

Joseph Jaworski, who gave courses in leadership in the eighties, became aware of the power of listening while talking to a friend about a question that was occupying his thoughts. He spoke of his experience in the following way:

> His listening enabled me to sort out and develop my thoughts. While I was speaking, his eyes never wandered. He looked me full in the face and gave me his undivided attention, as if nothing else mattered at that moment. The more he listened, the better I was able to formulate my thoughts and the surer I became of what I was saying. This experience with Anthony taught me a great deal about the power of listening and how important it is for helping leaders to dream, develop and express their visions of the future. When I spoke to him

at the time, a feeling of great peace and tranquillity came over me.[57]

You get this peace and tranquillity because inwardly things come into proportion, become clear and self-evident. You thus, in a deeper layer, gain insight into the problem and how to deal with it in the right way. It shows that you have connected to your spiritual Self. You can feel it too. It translates into the feeling of peace, harmony and inner strength that comes from such an experience.

By listening in this way as executive, you help your employee to connect to their inner core. That means helping the other to take the inner steps that lead to phase 4 or 5 in their personal development.

Relinquishing power and status

It is clear that this kind of leadership also has ethical aspects. The intentions with which you put yourself at the service of the other, your employee, must be sincere and you must consciously wish to enhance the development and autonomy of the other, both in the fulfilment of his task and in his humanity. That will only succeed if you recognize and can relinquish your ego-needs. These are, for instance, wanting to manage and control everything, using your power, diminishing the other in order to boost yourself in some way. These desires are not compatible with service. AES already discusses this when taking on a new executive. The company expects their executives to be of service to the employees and to relinquish their power voluntarily. Bakke, the CEO, emphasizes that such a question and step is no sinecure and must on no account be underestimated: 'I cannot emphasize enough how difficult that is, but it is the most crucial part of what we do.'[58] After all, it is natural that you gain power and prestige if you have had a certain education and have reached a certain position. Others acknowledge that and you come to expect it. Such patterns and expectations can only be shattered if the executive inwardly and actively chooses to do so.

In general, executives in phase 5 organizations attach little importance to power and status and have relatively low salaries and modest offices.

Spiritual leadership

Phase 5 leadership is, in fact, *spiritual leadership*. Why? Because, as executive, you concern yourself at all levels with development of the spirit. In the first place, you do this by stimulating everyone in the organization to concentrate on their core task, by seeing that everyone is aligned to the mission, values and principles, and by developing a vision. In the second place, you treat your employees in such a way that they are inwardly awakened. That is done by acknowledging their development as a human being, constantly appealing to their inner Self and thus helping them to become spiritually active. In this way, you help them develop their spiritual potential. This works best if you are conscious of it and inwardly make yourself serviceable to the other and their development.

From time immemorial, this approach is characteristic of spiritual leadership in all spiritual traditions, including eastern spirituality and western Christianity. Real spiritual growth in a person only occurs when another puts himself at the service of their development. This can be either a moment or a longer period of time. Indisputably, here again there is the aspect of an offer.

In the Chinese Book of Changes, the I Ching, the following comment is written on image 42: *The Increase*:

Real government should be service. An offer by the higher which brings about the increase of the lower is known as growth, thus indicating the spirit, which alone has the power to help the world.[59]

In this case, 'higher' does not only mean someone who is at a higher stage of spiritual development, but also someone who, through their knowledge and experience, is able to ask just that question or give that insight that the other needs at that moment. Service to the development of the other is expressed in the Bible in the image of Jesus Christ washing his disciples' feet:

> Jesus knowing that the Father had given all things into his hands, and that he was come from God and went to God; he riseth from supper, and laid aside his garments; and took a towel and girded himself.
> After that he poureth water into a basin, and began to wash the disciples' feet, and to wipe them with the towel wherewith he was girded.[60]

When the disciple Peter protests against this servile gesture, Jesus says: 'What I do thou knowest not now; but thou shalt know hereafter.' Meaning that there is a deeper reason behind the gesture which cannot be divulged at that moment.

The offer spoken of in the I Ching is about putting your ego aside, relinquishing ego-experiences and personal honour, and wanting to support the other in their development. Only then can the wisdom and insight-giving power of the spirit work in you and through you to help the other.

The more we become aware that all development in phase 5, whether it be that of the organization, the

employees or the executives, is in fact spiritual development, the more the spiritual element in leadership will be
acknowledged and stimulated.

Inner development of the executive
What does this demand of the executive himself? The
answer to this has really already been given.

The executive must not omit a single part of the personal
development process described before; he must build up a
good ego-feeling in phase 3, then go on through phase 4
and then develop his spiritual Self in phases 5 and 6. As
was shown in Part One, this demands, in the first place,
self-insight and self-management—self-leadership. You
only get self-insight by reflecting regularly on your own
thoughts, feelings and behaviour. This gives you self-
knowledge, knowledge of your strong and weak points
and how to deal with them. By doing so, you convert your
ego so that your higher spiritual Self gets room for
expression. A similar attitude of reflective attention and
inner activity is necessary in order to gain real insight into
what is happening in the world, in the organization and
between people and to discover what wants to happen
there. Besides, the executive in phases 4 and 5, and, of
course, in those following, must inwardly connect to the
spiritual world. It is, after all, from there that you get your
ideas and inspiration.

In order to develop the inner agility that allows you to
enter the spiritual world, you have to get to know that
world, study its laws and inwardly connect to the higher
forces at work there. Then these continue to work in you. It
is interesting to see that an increasing number of executives
are, besides their work, engaging in spiritual or religious
things. They read spiritually inspired books, meditate or

pray regularly and are strengthened by it. There are also ever more (top) executives who invite people to come to the organization to help them and the employees take steps on the spiritual path.

What I have said here is identical to what innovative thinkers, such as Peter Senge and Charles Kiefer, have noticed. Earlier on, at the end of phase 4, I mentioned that they find it characteristic of an organization in phase 5 that use is made of feeling and inspiration—the work of the spirit—next to reason and rational analysis.

Phase 6: The organization as a new community

Involvement and love

What does a phase 6 organization look like? It is not yet possible to give an extensive description, since we do not know how things will develop in the future. There are, however, a few elements that can be named. Where phase 5 was about realizing values and principles and the full inner independence of employees, the emphasis in phase 6 will be on our involvement with other people and their development—on love.

To the employee in this phase, the development of others is equally important, if not more so, than his or her own. This is because spiritual development is continuous. In phase 5, the spirit or the spiritual Self is mainly working in the employee as a person and shows in the wish to develop to the core, both personally and spiritually. This process continues in the individual in phase 6, but at the same time the workings of the spirit amongst people will also be seen, namely, in the way the employees relate to each other and collaborate. Just as we feel the need for our own development in phase 4 and 5, we will in phase 6 fully experience and feel the needs of the other and want to help and support her or him. We will experience this feeling towards the other as something that comes from the depths of our being. The terms 'need' and 'desire' then get a completely different shade and meaning to what we now give them. Our current needs and desires in relation to others come from our ego and that means that they are biased in such a way that we always also want something for ourselves. In phase 6, these impulses are totally targeted towards the other. That is because they emanate from our spiritual Self. This means that they are unselfish and free.

The executive as an example

We can imagine what will occur between employees in this phase 6. We can already see it in the relationship between executive and employee. The fundamental task of the executive – in particular in phase 5 – is his putting himself at the service of the employee. That is what it is all about. Any form of training or counselling of executives nowadays is aimed in that direction. In all sorts of ways, the executive is shown how to learn to know himself, to put his ego aside and to attune to the employee in such a way that the latter feels he is being really heard, seen and helped to take the next step – personally as well as professionally. This demands of the executive the courage to put his style of leadership up for discussion again and again. Through all that social abilities are developed and personal leadership put into practice. Only then can the executive be serviceable to his employees and their development in a free, unselfish and loving way.

The employee has a similar task. Initiatives for this

development can already be seen in, for instance, inter-
vision groups, where people freely discuss questions and
problems they come across in their work and personally
with the aim of helping each other. In phase 6, this will be
the normal way of working. The emphasis will be on sis-
terly and brotherly behaviour. This will bring about a new
feeling of solidarity – and love – amongst the employees in
the organization.

In phase 6, the aim will be to let this aspect of involvement and love run through all the layers of the organization as a principal value. Involvement and helping each
other in teams and departments will become normal,
because every employee is inwardly aware of the whole,
which can only develop and fulfil its task if individuals,
teams and departments contribute uniquely to that whole.
The result of these ideas and aims will be an entirely new
feeling of community in the organization.

Inner conflict
Does this mean that phase 6 will be in heavenly spheres?
Not at all. For, together with the increase of the light of the
spirit in and amongst people, so do the forces of darkness
increase. By nature they work in the unconscious and as
yet untransformed parts of our ego, which are still very
much present in phase 6. Their reality will become
apparent in an unprecedented increase of phenomena such
as egotism, selfishness, violence and lack of love. We will
all come across them constantly, in ourselves and in our
relationships. We can already see them at work everywhere, especially in those organizations that introduced
and stimulates the competition element in all layers. This
arouses not the good qualities in employees, but the
egotistical, negative sides. The result is an atmosphere that

makes people ill. Such experiences, however, do have a place. Real love which comes from the core can only be developed by experiencing what egotism, harshness and lack of love mean, and how that works out, both in yourself and in others. Only then can you really choose how you want to behave and what you stand for.

The phases 5, 6 and 7 will therefore only develop positively if we learn to know and deal with the dark forces working in ourselves, in other people and in our relationships with each other. It is there that the inner conflict will escalate in all its fury, the battle between the forces of evil, which do not want human development to continue to higher levels of consciousness, and those of light and love, which want progress. This will require continual inner activity, reflection, self-knowledge and, as I said, conscious choices.

'Love' in phase 6 is not about having nice, positive feelings towards all other people, but a spiritual strength which inwardly, constantly and consciously has to be won from the shady, negative sides, the 'undelivered' part of yourself. Only then can it become a free, giving force of love, working towards the other and the good in the world.

Phase 7: The organization as contributor to world development

The greater whole

As in phase 6, it is difficult to describe the phase 7 organization. I can only name a number of aspects that will play a role.

In phase 7, the organization aims in particular at the contribution it wants to make to the development of the

greater whole. Here again we see that spiritual development in people always continues. While the emphasis on
the development of awareness lay on the personal in phase
5 and on relationships with others in phase 6, we see that
awareness and effort of organizations in phase 7 are aimed
at care for, and further development of, the greater whole
of which we are part: society, mankind, nature, the earth,
the world, the cosmos.

We can already see signs of phase 7 in our day. During
the past 25 years, we have become very aware of the
dangers threatening our planet and its people. Not only do
we have today weapons of mass destruction that could
wipe out the earth and mankind many times over, we have
also realized how much technological and industrial welfare has been at the expense of nature and mankind these
past 50 years. Primeval forests are cut down on a huge
scale, seas overfished, resources used up, ground and
water polluted and people in Third World countries used
as cheap labour. This is the result of a way of thinking and
acting that wants to make profits at any cost. It shows what
the materially orientated phase 3 thinking of individual
people and organizations can lead to.

Sustainable enterprise

In the past ten years, another way of thinking is emerging
in a number of organizations as a result of their leaders
developing individually to phase 4 and 5. When the
organization then makes the step to phases 4 and 5 and
quality, values and principles become its basis, it starts on
'sustainable enterprise'. Sustainable enterprise means that
its aim is to bring and keep economic, social and ecological
interests in equilibrium.

In 1996, Ray Anderson, top man of Interface, a world

leader in carpet tiles in Scherpenzeel (Netherlands), got the idea of, as he said, no longer exploiting his own planet. Since then, sustainable enterprise has the highest priority in the company. It aims to be completely sustainable within 20 years. Already, all waste is recycled and the factories in England and Ireland are run entirely on solar and wind energy. The factory in Scherpenzeel will soon follow. Further, the company is replacing nylon, which is the main component of the carpets, with 'socially acceptable' material. They are trying to make carpets from maize starch and are intensively researching potatoes and sugar-beet as possible raw materials for carpets. Anderson: 'It has cost a lot of time and money and at first the product will also become a bit more expensive. But if the raw materials are common, the investment will repay itself.'[61]

Gradually, there are more companies taking the step towards phase 5. In the Netherlands, the so-called Nido-project was started: 'from financial to sustainable returns'.[62] There are over 20 larger companies in the Netherlands who want to be a sustainable enterprise. Such companies do not want to overtax or pollute the environment. They replace the raw materials they use (by planting trees, for example), and build schools and clinics in local communities in the Third World to compensate the people for their work.

Various stages of awareness

It is obvious that one can differentiate various stages of awareness in the relationship of a company to a greater whole — the community, mankind, the earth, the world. These stages of awareness in turn are related to development in the different phases.

In the traditional organization in phase 2 there is no, or

hardly any, reference to pollution or misuse of raw materials. In phase 3, together with industrial and technological developments, pollution of the environment and
the unlimited use of mineral and vegetable raw materials
begins. In companies developing through phase 4, 5 and 6,
there is growing awareness that this cannot go on. On the
basis of certain values and principles, things will be done
differently and the company becomes a sustainable enterprise. At first, this often looks like phase 3 thinking and
doing. The thinking is: if I invest now in environmentally
friendly solutions, I will later profit the more. But then,
here and there, the next phase of conscious action starts.
Inwardly, the leadership of the company and a growing
number of employees feel the desire to contribute to the
greater whole, even though it brings no advantage, even
though it costs the organization money. In this sort of
awareness, the development towards phase 7 can be seen,
the phase in which the current values are expressed in all
the layers of the organization, both inwardly and to the
outer world. In other words, companies in phase 7 will not
only be based on certain values and principles but will take
it for granted that they contribute in a conscious, free and
unselfish way to the welfare and development of society,
mankind, nature, and will include this qualitative thinking
in their mission. Through their inner spiritual development, the employees in those organizations will feel and
know: Whoever we are as people, wherever we live and
work, essentially we form one whole with other people,
with nature, with the earth and with the world as a whole.
That which lives in me, lives in them and what lives in
them lives in me. The one cannot be without the other. We
need each other to contribute to each other's development
and to achieve that for which we are on earth.

11. Conclusions and Overview

In more than one phase at a time

Like an individual, an organization can also be in more than one phase at a time. A company could give attention to values and principles so that it looks is if it is in phase 5, while the management is still directing on hierarchic principles and controls things as in phases 2 and 3. Whether the company is mainly in phase 3 or 5 can only be determined by the phenomena that get the emphasis. For a company too, there is the task of becoming aware of the bits that have been left behind and developing them. It is very confusing and even leads to disorientation if parts of the organization do not keep pace with each other and differ too much.

In phase 5 or in phase 2?

An organization sometimes presents itself in a way that is reminiscent of phase 5. If one looks closely, however, one notices characteristics that stand in the way of the new impulses belonging to the further stages.

An example of this is the international bank BCCI (Bank of Credit and Commerce International), founded in 1972 in the Middle East. The company's philosophy was expressed by the term 'natural management'.[63] I use the word 'was' because the bank went bankrupt in later years.

Natural management was inspired by the laws of nature and saw an organization as an eco-system. At BCCI this meant that the aim was to conform to nature, and great value was put on values and principles such as spontaneity, trust, initiative, intuition and feelings. While these values and principles were given priority as far as possible, not so much attention was paid to structure. Although not against it, structure was limited as far as possible in order to give space to the values and principles. Thus there was no formal planning, no conventional plan of operation or conventional budgeting. In BCCI's view, this constantly changes according to the interchange between people. The company made use of verbal agreements and called that 'dynamic planning'.

As is the case with companies in phase 5, the emphasis in this bank was on people and their development. To BCCI, management was not for 'getting something done with the aid of people'. That put the emphasis on the work and not on the people that did the work. According to them, management is 'the art of development of people by means of work'. They said it was by chance that the company was a bank. It could well have been something else. The main thing was people's development and the bank was just a means to that end. In itself, this is a very interesting idea which certainly deserves a place in phase 5.

But now the other side of the coin. As an eco-system, this organization was aimed at unification of its staff. They saw this unification as an active growth and development process, made possible by the work. The process of unification was all-important. 'By unification the people make the development of the bank possible.'[64] Each member of staff was considered to be a member of the family — an often used term — and manager and executive of the company. Through this family-feeling and the emphasis on unification, very little room was left for individual achievement. The word 'I' sounded arrogant to BCCI ears. A senior manager: 'We like to share the honours. Nobody needs to know who has done something. That is not important. It is a communal achievement.'[65]

BCCI's emphasis therefore was on the group, not on the individual. The individual did not count. This means that with this aspect the emphasis was on phase 2.

BCCI provides a good example of an organization that, on the one hand, brings something new — management is the art of development of people by means of work — but, on the other hand, so completely negates the individual aspect that they return to an earlier phase of development. That must in the end have created chaos. It shows how important it is to know the laws of development in people and organizations.

The position of the individual

The position of the individual is the criterion for determining the development phase of the organization. As the phase-model on page 122 shows — and as can also be seen in everyday life — the main thing in the first part of the evolution of mankind is, in the first instance, the development of the 'I', the self-awareness of the individual. From this individual self-awareness, developing especially in phases 3, 4 and 5, completely new connections are made to a person's inner world, other people and to the world around.

It is important that phase 4 and 5 companies realize this. If they do not, the emphasis in the organization will soon be back in phase 2 again, especially if the company's aim is unification as in BCCI. An organization only really reaches phase 5 when executives and most of the employees stand in themselves, are connected to their inner Self, and can from there say 'yes' to the mission, vision, values and principles of the company and also realize these in their structure and actions. Each employee in a phase 5 organization has their own place and is responsible for their own decisions and achievements. Everything in phase 5 thus has to be made the person's 'own' and 'personally valid'.

Pioneering phase, professionalization phase and transformation phase

In Part Two of this book, I described the development phases of relationships and groups. I said that one could see the corresponding laws working through time, but that they can also be found in the development of new relationships or teams. It is the same in the development of organizations. The development sketched by me in this book has taken place in organizations for centuries and will continue to do so. It is inherent in the development we people go through.

The development phases, however, are also valid for the foundation of each new company and show the growth from phase to phase which each company must go through. These phases have different names.

A new company begins with what is generally called a pioneering phase and, after a time, moves on to a professionalization phase. The pioneering phase corresponds to what I described in phase 2 of organization development. The new organization has one or more founders who have the ideas about what and how things should be done. They are the boss. Some soon take other people on, others do the work themselves at first. Characteristic of this phase is that everyone, from high to low, does what needs doing as a matter of course. If the services or products of the company catch on and the organization expands, more people are taken on. After a time, it becomes necessary to divide the tasks and develop systems and procedures to make things manageable.

Sometimes the pioneering phase is artificially extended — even if it is no longer really possible — in order to emphasize the cosiness and feelings of comradeship and collectivity that are characteristic of the pioneering phase (and phase 2). One knows or feels that the atmosphere in the next phase, the professionalization phase (phase 3), will be different. Through the division of tasks and functions and the establishment of systems and procedures, there will be a certain commercialization and coolness. All this creates distance between people. The result is that they need to find a new relationship to each other. It is, for instance, in an organization in the professionalization phase no longer possible for everyone to just walk into the founder's office as one used to do. Employees who continue to do so get confused and conflicts may occur.

Sooner or later, however, the step from the pioneering phase towards phase 3, the professionalization phase, has to be made if the company is to continue to exist. And after a time it will again be necessary, through the inner growth of executives and employees, to move on to the phases 4 and 5.

Today, most of the companies founded during the last few decades are, for the greater part, in phase 3.

The development-line of employees

It is interesting to look at the development of employees through the various phases of development. What is the general line?

If we go back to phase 1 in ancient Egypt, we see that there is no room for an individual worker who makes his own choices. Everyone felt at one with everybody and everything and especially with the all-supporting godly principle personified in the priest-king. Then, in phase 2, there is a process of separation in which the distance to the world of the gods becomes greater and you come down to earth. In phases 2 and 3, as employee in the service of others, you gradually awaken. You become conscious that you are an individual, with your own thoughts, feelings and needs. In phases 1, 2 and 3, you are guided by others from the outside. At first, somebody else determines and decides everything for you, until they acknowledge you as an independent person. From that moment on, they work with you and support you in your own development as a person and as an employee.

Next, in phase 4, both you and the organization go through a process of transformation. In phase 5, the executive's support makes such an appeal to your inner core that you take the helm yourself. This opens the way to personal leadership. You are responsible for your own work processes and the collaboration with others. The executive, who first directed everything from above, is now next to you as coach — not to tell you what to do, but as discussion-partner in the process of reflection on yourself and your work. In practice, this is now a relationship of equals.

Thus a line can be seen in the development of the

employee which begins in a condition of unawareness, and is followed by the development of awareness of his or her own person and connection to the inner Self, which leads to self-guidance, personal leadership and to ever-increasing responsibility and authority.

The development-line of leadership

Again, in order to see the general line, we must go back to the organization in phase 1. The leadership of the priest-king is still transpersonal. It is entirely at the service of God or the world of the gods and has no personal element. In phase 2, leadership has been divorced from its connection to the divine and has gradually come down to earth. Instead of looking upwards, the attention is now more on earthly reality, on the work that needs to be done and the people who do it. In directing people and work in phase 2, the personal 'I' of the executive develops. This development continues in phase 3, but halfway through something special happens. Somehow the executive becomes aware of his employee as an independent person, with his own opinions and behaviour. He realizes that his former method of directing and controlling from above no longer works and that the employee needs something else for his development. The executive puts him- or herself at the service of the development of his employee and helps him in his development towards greater independence. Finally, in phase 5, when transcending his or her own self, the executive gives the employee the right to make their own decisions and carry responsibility and authority. By doing so he relinquishes the remnants of his power.

The following line can be seen through the various

phases in the development of leadership. First there is the supra-personal leadership given by God. Secondly the leadership becomes personal. And finally through the transformation process, it offers service, so that the element of leadership can develop in the employee.

The same sort of line is found in the aspect of power. First, power is supra-personal, then personal and finally — in phase 5 and after—relinquished and passed on to the employee.

Another interesting aspect is that you can see that the executive, as far as his social capacities are concerned, is usually one step ahead of the employee's development. When the employee is in phase 2, the executive is for the greater part in phase 3 and so on. In phase 5, when the executive, as coach, puts himself at the service of the work and budding leadership of the employee, he develops in himself those qualities and capabilities which belong to phase 6.

12. The Phases of Development in an Ideal-based Organization

In chapter 10, the development road of commercial organizations was described. Now it is the turn of ideal-based organizations.

Why this special description? Because, although ideal-based organizations go through the same phases as commercial ones, they do that in a different way. If one is to understand the ideal-based organization, it is important to see in how far the laws described work in it too.

Ideal-based organizations differ fundamentally on a number of points. In contrast to commercial organizations, their primary aim is not that of profit-making, but the realization of an ideal. Since profit-making is not their first priority, they are often called 'non-profit' organizations. Ideal-based organizations are founded by one or more people with an ideal, a strong conviction or a truth as their starting-point. By their existence and work they want to contribute to the development and improvement of the world. Their mission usually makes this clear. Amnesty International for instance describes as its mission:

> Amnesty International is an independent and impartial organization pursuing the observance of the Universal Declaration of Human Rights.
>
> Amnesty International campaigns for ending grave abuses of the right to life, the right not to be tortured, the right to freedom of conscience and expression, and the right to freedom from discrimination.

The mission of an ideal-based organization is primarily

aimed at changing the world or society. That of commercial organizations is also aimed at society, but contains a lot of wording in which profit-making is the central aim.

Another important difference between a commercial and an ideal-based organization is that the latter has its ideal mission from its foundation, mostly started in phase 2, while the former only develops it in phase 5.

Ideal-based organizations include such socially committed institutions as Friends of the Earth, the World Wildlife Fund, Medicins sans Frontières, as well as political parties and ideological institutions such as churches or other institutions with a spiritual aim.

How does the path of ideal-based organizations develop through the various phases? Here, too, phase 1 is the prelude. The following is a summary.

1. The theocratic phase

Society—and thus also the work relationship between people—was characterized in ancient Egypt by the central position of the priest-king as the intermediary between the world of the gods and the people on earth. He was the executor of divine will in the world, with an almost godly status. Society was completely theocratically structured and entirely hierarchic. Everything belonged to the Pharaoh—people, their lives, their land and its harvest. At that time, there was no individual human awareness. People felt themselves part of a larger whole that covered the entire earth and was guided and inspired by the gods.

2. The autocratic or pioneering phase

In phase 2, the autocratic or pioneering phase of an ideal-based organization—more than in phase 2 of a commercial one—something of phase 1 is still at work. After all, an idealistic organization is about ideals and therefore spiritual by nature. How does this show itself?

Leadership

In an ideal-based phase 2 organization, there is usually one person who takes the lead. This could be the founder, but also someone from the founding group or the group that succeeded the founder. It is always someone who can put the ideal into words well, who can appeal to the inner person and who knows which way to go to reach the goal. In a political party, for instance, such a person is the personification of the party's ideal and policy: the way in which the group handles the ideal and wants to realize it. Jan Marijnissen, one of the founders of the (Dutch) Socialist Party, party-leader and chairman of the party in Parliament, is such a man. He is described as someone with the gift of the gab, who can bring and sell his message well. A journalist says of him: 'He really is what they say: very clever, well-read, with an instinct for the right moment and, of course, with the gift of the gab.'[66] Asked whether there would have been an SP without Marijnissen, he says: 'Difficult to say. With only Marijnissen there would have been no SP. It is just the group. But only the group without Marijnissen? I doubt things would have turned out as they did.'[67] In the same way, other organizations and ideal-based institutions have leaders or leading groups who personify the ideal or truth and keep it in trust, at the same time giving guidance to the resulting work and the people involved. There is still something of the magic and power of the past at work around such leaders, who take care of both the spiritual and earthly elements, as did the priest-king in olden days.

Everybody and everything in the service of the ideal
Inspiring leaders and ideals draw people who devote their heart and soul to the cause, both employees and volunteers. There is often a certain emotional dependence on the leader. For the members or employees, he personifies something sublime because he proclaims values and truths which are very real to them but which they cannot put into words themselves. This complete dedication to the ideal means that executives of the SP have for years been out every evening, bringing the party paper round, and are satisfied with a low salary or even work for nothing. Such dedication can also be found in other ideal-based organizations. A woman who exchanged her job in a commercial organization for that of campaign-leader with Greenpeace, says: 'Here you do not think about noting down quarters of an hour. You work far too long hours anyway. You work from your own motivation. I do not talk about my work with Greenpeace, but about my life with Greenpeace. Now I have tasted this, I cannot imagine ever going back to the commercial sector.'[68]

Working together for the realization of an ideal creates a strong bond between the members or employees. There is a strong community spirit and a very obvious group culture with its own specific values, norms and basic principles. Characteristic of an ideal-based organization in phase 2 is that the employees or members appreciate each other for the way in which the other is able to express the ideal or conviction in words and/or deeds. In phase 2, everybody and everything is subservient to the realization of the ideal. The personal element, however, such as personal needs or differing opinions of employees, has little or no place at all.

3. The professional or bureaucratic phase

As the organization expands and the number of employees grows, it also goes through the development of phase 3, the professional or bureaucratic phase. In chapter 10, I showed that phase 3 organizations have two new developments: that of the ego-element and that of the physical instrument, the structure. The 'I'-element can be recognized in the division of work into tasks and duties, decentralization into departments, the leadership of the executive and the development of the 'I'-personality of the employees working in the organization. The physical element comes from the development of the structure: systems and procedures which support, coordinate and manage the various work-processes. So in phase 3, management gives the organization new forms and structures so that it can develop further.

Resistance to change
In ideal-based organizations, the step from phase 2 to phase 3 is often problematical. Often the change does not work well for a number of reasons. In the first place, nearly all attention and energy is given to the aims *outside* the organization and not much thought is given to internal processes. Secondly, the executives see themselves in phase 2 more as keepers of the ideal, and therefore of the status quo, rather than as managers of work and change-processes. In many cases, they also miss the necessary affinity and skills. Thirdly, the employees in an ideal-based organization often have an almost instinctive resistance to material things, such as money and finances, or the design of work-processes by structures, systems and management. This resistance is, on the one hand, due to fear that

the free way of working, in which everyone does more or less as he pleases, will no longer be possible. On the other hand, they fear that they will end up in a straitjacket of systems, procedures and management measures which curb their freedom and suppress spontaneity and creativity. Knowing what goes on in commercial organizations fills many employees in an ideal-based organization with horror. They have often left their job and come to this one for that very reason.

'We (!) don't want to become an efficient organization!' an angry employee shouted during a meeting in which problems arising from vague procedures were discussed. Since they do not clearly choose for the shaping of physical structures in the organization, many ideal-based organizations continue to work in their inefficient and even chaotic way.

(Further) training of employees in leadership and management skills is omitted. This leads to the prolongation of long meetings in which vague decisions are made. Clear choices about tasks and authority are also neglected, because there is resistance against hierarchic structures. The division of roles and positions remain vague. Employees receive different salaries for the same work. The lack of clear vision and long-term policy results in decisions being made one month and reversed the next. There are many other examples. Employees tend to take the chaos, the vagueness and the extra effort these cost them daily into the bargain, as long as they have sufficient energy for them and find the work worthwhile.

A woman who came from a commercial organization to become office-coordinator with the (equivalent of the) RSPCA, noticed on arrival how many things were not properly organized. It was even chaotic. But, she says, she likes it: 'I put up with it because I believe in what I am doing.'[69]

Personal attention and guidance

Apart from the physical, structural elements, the 'I'-element also gets very little attention in ideal-based organizations. By this I mean the personal and professional development of the individual employee. As we have seen in previous chapters, the employee in phase 3 wants to become visible personally; he wants to present himself and develop himself further, both personally and professionally. This requires help and guidance from an executive who acknowledges these needs and can structure them. This help is important because employees in this phase also want to take the step towards the phase of ego-development and independence in their personal lives.

Here we come to the second problem area in ideal-based organizations. Within the institution or company there is usually little awareness or room for these personal and professional needs of the employees. Besides, the executives often lack vision and skills in this area, since the organization as a community is on the whole still in phase 2. Many ideal-based organizations are shocked when they realize they are in this situation and at first have great difficulty in admitting it. Because of the strongly developed community spirit, they think they are in phase 6 rather than in phase 2. After some time, however, they realize that the organization has all the characteristics of phase 2 and that no steps for further development have been taken. Attention has all the time been focused on the supra-personal: the realization of convictions, the ideal, the truth, to which the personal element is subservient. Transformation in the relationship between employees or members, such as takes place in commercial organizations in phase 3, therefore does not occur easily in these institutions or companies. Here, in this phase, we seldom find executives who dedicate themselves to the development of independence of individual members or employees. This means that most ideal-based organizations — but there are, of course, exceptions — continue working in phase 3 as if they are in phase 2. At best, adaptations are made here and there.

4. The transformation phase

Getting stuck
If there is no timely renewal, an organization becomes rigid, especially one with an idealistic basis. If there is no development, we see the original loose and enthusiastic culture gradually being replaced by a coercive one. The emphasis shifts from the values to often unconscious norms. While everyone at first supported the ideals and knew 'this is our goal and that is what we want to realize', we now see that ideas of how or how not to behave come into being as unconscious norms. This process is very slow and inconspicuous; it can only be recognized by good evaluation. Nuances disappear and starting-points are stated in increasingly black and white terms.[70] Criticism from inside and outside the organization is ignored or dismissed as hostile. This is not surprising. Criticism is a threat to the feeling of unity and unanimity to which one is so attached in phase 2. Employees or members must adapt to the existing culture or leave if they do not want to do so. If these problems occur the executives often show their influence more strongly than before and tighten the reins.

They do this because they fear for the loss of their own position and the ideal or the loss of the continuity of the organization, society or party. This fear and the incapacity to meet the crisis professionally make them little inclined to listen to things that do not fit into their own framework. This often makes their actions conservative, repressive and sometimes even manipulative. The atmosphere becomes insecure, mutual trust disappears and power-games and conflicts prevail, a development which many employees find hard to take. Not only may they be shocked by the leader's behaviour, or that of other executives, which is often a flagrant contradiction of the ideal, but they are also afraid that both the ideal and the party, society or organization which meant so much to them will cease to exist. After a time, a number of them cannot bear it any longer and quit, while others adapt even more to the existing culture or rebel.

Thus, during a crisis within the (Dutch) Labour Party in 2000, a number of members demanded clarity about the aims of the party. Did it want to be a broad party with strong roots in society, as it used to be? Or did it want to continue as a 'narrow' party, in which a select little group made the decisions and the members only had the role of donor? It was clear to these members that the party leaders did not want critical members. This, and the fact that the critical younger members had already left, meant, they reasoned, that the dissolution of the party was already set in motion.[71]

If the processes in the institution, society or party become rigid and life goes out of it to a great extent, a lot of energy is lost in the outward maintenance of the organization. Much less energy is then given to the realization of the ideal itself. This leads to the danger of a negative spiral.

Members and employees turn their backs on the institution, church or society and it then turns out to be difficult to fill the open places at short notice. The situation becomes more and more difficult for those left behind because the work has to be done with fewer people and under less pleasant circumstances, without a positive result as compensation. Sooner or later this will mean the end of the organization.

Transformation

Is there any future in such a situation? Certainly there is, at least if there is a real wish for change. This begins when a number of executives and employees or members decide that this can no longer go on and that they want to go through a transformation process (phase 4) together. That means that they are prepared to recognize the situation by naming it and to make a clean sweep by learning to do things differently and changing the culture.

In general, this cannot be done without outside help. This help is important because everyone is personally far too caught up in the existing relationships and behaviour patterns, making it difficult to take distance and design a new approach themselves. This will often mean that a new manager, an interim-executive or an organization-coach is appointed. The organization must, in fact, go through the same process as that described in phase 4 for commercial organizations. In this situation it is necessary to evaluate well and to cope with the experiences in the past in such a way that the feeling of security and trust gradually returns. On the other hand a vision towards the future must be developed and values and principles formulated that will form the basis of the organization in phases 4 and 5. In order to avoid repeating myself, please see the paragraphs

The transformation process, Clearing up the past, From focus on results to focus on people and *Metanoia* of phase 4 in chapter 10.

Completing the development of phase 3

All these changes, however, will only be effective if the organization picks up the tasks in phase 3 that got left behind. Without a good physical instrument, it will not have a solid foundation and the transformation of phase 4 will not be able to take place.

Ideal-based organizations that still want to wind up phase 3 properly must choose a structure that suits their identity and opt for the development of management skills and leadership qualities, in particular with reference to communication and decision-making.

Many ideal-based organizations that got stuck in the last few years are now developing in phase 3. It is not an easy time for them. Their members or employees miss the old feeling of unanimity, which, though sometimes insecure and restricted, also offered safety. The new developments are felt to be cool and distant. Besides this, there is the fear that the ideal they support will be lost. Since people are not used to thinking in terms of development processes, they often think that this new phase is a lasting one.

There is a danger that ideal-based organizations that want to complete phase 3 properly forget the collaboration with their employees or members, thus paying insufficient attention to the 'I'-element. Unfortunately, this occurs all too often. For instance, a new structure or completely new policy is introduced, or a new director is appointed, without the employees or members having had any say in the matter. In effect, the controlling power from above from phase 2 is continued, but now on the management level!

From focus on the ideal to focus on the individual

For the further development of the ideal-based organization, it is fundamental that, in phase 3, the emphasis is
shifted to the individual employees or members of the
society or party and to their individual contribution. That
is necessary for good further development of the organization in the later phases. After all, in phase 5, besides the
organization's own task, the *person* — employee or member
— *as individual is central*, so that he or she can contribute
from their core, their own values and principles, *in their
own way* to the development of the organization and the
realization of the ideal. In phase 4, the transformation
phase, there is therefore a change of policy. The focus on
the supra-personal ideal is shifted to the focus on the
individual person, the individual employee, the individual
member and her or his spiritual awakening. For from
phase 4, *all new development* comes from the inner spiritual
being of the individual.

Transformation of the ideal

What does this development mean for the ideal? In practice, you see that — up to phase 4 — the ideal has always
existed in a supra-personal way and now, back in phase 3,
it disappears into the background. This process continues
as the step from phase 3 to phase 4 is taken. Sometimes the
ideal seems dead, as there is so little left of it. It depends on
the alertness of the leadership and the responsible individual employees and members whether the organization
can develop further and reach the challenges of phase 5. If
not, it will succumb in phase 4 and with it the ideal.
Developing through the transformation of phase 4 is going
through the eye of the needle.

An organization that does reach phase 5 demonstrates

that it has, in all its facets, gone through the transformation process and that the ideal is expressed in an entirely new way in the organization itself and in most of the individual employees or members. This, of course, demands attention to training, development and awakening of the individuals working in the organization. If this succeeds, the ideal, the truth, the conviction will be established in a new way in the hearts and souls of those involved. In phase 3, the organization, as bearer of the ideal, was founded in the physical — the structural — element, whereas in phase 5 this ideal has to find its basis in the spirit of the people involved. Only then do the individuals connect from their own inner core with the newly formulated ideal. And only then can a contribution be made towards the development of other people in phase 6 and the organization and society as a whole in phase 7.

Phases 5, 6 and 7

At the beginning of this chapter, I mentioned that commercial and ideal-based organizations go through the development phases in a different way. Where do they differ and where do they concur?

In the commercial organization, the road is followed from phase 1, the level of the supra-personal spirit, via the personal road and the materialistically focused phase 3 and the transformation phase 4 to the step towards the inner spirit in phase 5. In the ideal-based organization, the supra-personal element of the spirit is not only present in phase 1, but also in phase 2 and, for the greater part, also in phase 3. Only in phase 4 does a change take place. One becomes aware that an important element of development has been left out. This means that the organization must first deal with its 'forgotten bits' and as yet develop its physical and personal elements. Only then can the transformation process in phase 4 be completed and finally, in phase 5, the ideals reformulated out of the inner being of the individuals.

This shows that *both roads come together in phase 5*, the phase in which the individual becomes inwardly spiritually active. From phase 5 the path in the ideal-based organization develops in the same way as in the commercial organization. In the end both take the same road towards phases 6 and 7.

Comparison with the male and female road

Finally, I want to mention another interesting point. If you look closely, you will see that a commercial organization follows the development road of the man, while the ideal-based organization follows the development road of the female. In the latter too, the ego-phase (3) is less developed, so that the woman in the phase 4 process must first return to phase 3 for her own ego-development, before being able to go through phase 4 properly and connect to her inner spirit in phase 5.

This again shows that development processes in our personal lives, in relationships and in organizations are not fortuitous. They demonstrate that there is a mysterious deeper wisdom, not only connecting everything with everything but also giving it sense and meaning.

Spirit
primeval source of all being

visible in Nature with its wisdom, beauty and coherence,
active as a source of development for people and organizations,
awareness in man as a free and independent individual,
so that he, as bearer of the inner light of awareness
contributes lovingly to the development of his fellow-men
in the service of humanity, earth and cosmos
on the path to ever higher levels of awareness and existence.

Notes

Foreword

i   Teillard de Chardin, *The Phenomenon of Man*, Harper & Row, New York, 1961.

ii   In Beck, D.E., and Cowan, C.C., *Spiral Dynamics. Mastering Values, Leadership and Change*, Blackwell Publishers Ltd, Oxford, l996.

iii Steiner, Rudolf, *The Philosophy of Freedom*, Rudolf Steiner Press, London.

iv Teillard de Chardin, op. cit.

v   Graves, C.W., in Beck, D.E., and Cowan, C.C., op. cit.

vi Tyll van de Voort holds and M.Sc. in Management Development from the University of Bristol. He currently lives in Camphill Community at Oaklands Park, Newham-on-Severn, in Southwest England.

1. Jung, Carl Gustav, *Die Beziehungen zwischen dem Ich und dem Unbewussten* (The Relationship between the 'I' and the Subconscious), p. 263, Walter Verlag, Olten, Switzerland.

2. *Jonas Magazine*, April 2000.

3. Pouw, Cathrien A., *De ontwikkeling van leiderschap* (The Development of Leadership), Interstudie, Arnhem, 1994.

4. Interview in *Trouw* (Dutch daily newspaper), 12 October 2000.

5. May, Rollo, *Man's Search for Himself*, Souvenir Press, New York.

6. Covey, Stephen R., *The 7 Habits of Highly Effective People*, Simon & Schuster, New York.

7. Carl Gustav Jung pointed out that we must not confuse the 'ordinary I' and the Self: the former is identical to egocentricity and auto-eroticism. Self, however, includes far more than just an 'I'. It is just as much he or the others as I. See *Von*

den Wurzeln de Bewusstseins (On the Roots of Consciousness), p. 595, Walter Verlag, Olten, Switzerland.

8. Jung, Carl Gustav, article 'Bewusstsein, Unbewusste und Individuation' (Consciousness, Subconsciousness and Individualization) in: *Zentralblatt für Psychotherapie* (Central Periodical for Psychotherapy), 1939, p. 257.

9. Brug, Jos van der, *Levensfasen en werk, coachen, leidinggeven, teamwork* (Life-phases and Work, Coaching, Leadership, Teamwork), Indigo, Zeist 2000.

10. Knibbe, Hans, article 'De kunst van in-relatie-zijn' (The Art of being in a Relationship), in *Cirkel* (periodical Circle).

11. From *Info 3, Monatsmagazin für Spiritualität und Zeitfragen* (Monthly Magazine for Spirituality and Current Affairs), article 'Gewaltiger Zukunft' (Violent Future), no. 10, 1997.

12. Trungpa, Chögyam, *The Myth of Freedom and the Way of Meditation*, Shambala Publications, Boston.

13. Gray, John, *Men, Women and Relationships – Making Peace with the Opposite Sex*, Beyond Words, Oregon, USA.

14. Gädeke, Wolfgang, *Sexuality, Partnership and Marriage from a Spiritual Perspective*, Temple Lodge 1998.

15. Glöckler, Michaela, *Die männliche und weibliche Konstitution* (The Male and Female Constitution), Urachhaus, Stuttgart, 1968.

16. See note 13.

17. Rubin, Lilian B., *Intimate Strangers*, Harper & Row, New York.

18. See note 17.

19. Interview in *Jonas Magazine*, 30 May 1997.

20. In *Docta Ingnorantia*, quoted in Ekkehard Meffert, *Nicolaus von Kues, sein Lebensgang, seine Leere vom Geist* (Nicolaus von Kues, his Life, his Doctrine of the Spirit), Verlag Freies Geistesleben, Stuttgart, 1982.

21. Schuurman, C.J., *De medemens en wij* (Fellow Man and Us), Ankh-Hermes, Deventer, 1982.

22. Brink, Margarete van den, *More Precious than Light*, Hawthorn Press, Stroud, 1995.

23. Steiner, Rudolf, *Anthroposocial Leading Thoughts*, Rudolf Steiner Press, London, 1973.
24. Scott Peck, M., *The Different Drum*, Arrow Books, London, 1990.
25. See note 6.
26. Idem.
27. Idem.
28. Dongen, Mark van, *Excellent leidingeven* (Excellent Leadership), Academic Servire, Schoonhoven, 2001.
29. Siethoff, Hellmut J. ten, *Mehr Erfolg durch Soziales Handeln* (More Success through Social Dealing), Urachhaus, Stuttgart, 1996.
30. See note 24.
31. Gibran, Kahlil, *The Prophet*, Alfred A. Knopf Publishers, New York, 1945.
32. *Avanta Magazine*, June 1998.
33. *Avanta Magazine*, March 1999.
34. See note 6.
35. Johnson, Robert A., *Contentment*, Harper, San Francisco.
36. *Trouw*, 24 February 1998.
37. Schuit, Lenette, *De kracht van bezieling. Drijfveren van individuen en organisaties* (The Strength of Inspiration. Motives of Individuals and Organizations), Scriptum Management Lannoo, Tiel, 1999.
38. Kotter, John P., *Leading Change*, Harvard Business School Press, Boston.
39. Witteloostuijn, A. van, '*Après nous le déluge, De economie van de egocentrische hebzucht*' from: H. Schenk (ed.), *Repositioning of Companies* (Utrecht, 2001). A publication by the Koninklijke Vereniging voor de Staathuishoudkunde, Utrecht.
40. Huele, F.H., 'Transformatie Management: een discontinu proces' (Transformation management: a discontinuing process). In *Baakbericht* 157, Jan./Feb. 1999.
41. O'Reilly, Charles A., Pfeffer, Jeffrey, *Hidden Value. How Great*

Companies Achieve Extraordinary Results with Ordinary People, Harvard Business School Press, Boston, 2000.

42. Lier Marjan van (ed.), *Wat bezielt* ... (What possessed ...) Stichting Carnac, Amsterdam, 1996.

43. Overdijk, Carien, 'Marike van Lier Lels: "Arrogantie staat me tegen"' (Marike van Lier Lels: Arrogance palls on me), *Qui Vive* 2, 1998.

44. See note 41.

45. See Adams, John, *Transforming Work*, Miles River Press, Alexandria.

46. Partially derived from: John Adams, *Transforming Work*, see note 45.

47. See note 41.

48. Idem.

49. Idem.

50. Whitmore, John, *Coaching for Performance*, Nic. Brealey Publishing, London.

51. Investigation by International Survey Research, in: *Managersonline*, 10 September 2001.

52. See note 45.

53. See note 41.

54. Idem.

55. Idem.

56. Greenleaf, Robert, *Servant Leadership: A Journey into the Nature of Ligitimate Power and Greatness*, Paulist Press, New York.

57. Jaworski, Joseph, *Synchronicity. The Inner Path of Leadership*, Berrett-Koehler Publishers, San Francisco.

58. See note 41.

59. Baynes, Cary Fink/Richard Wilhelm, *The I Ching or Book of Changes*. Routledge & Paul Kegan, London.

60. The Bible, John 13:2.

61. *Trouw*, 10 November 2001.

62. Nido means: Nationaal initiatief duurzame ontwikkeling (National Initiative for Sustainable Development).

63. Adams, John, *Transforming Leadership*, Miles River Press, Alexandria.
64. Idem.
65. Idem.
66. Slager, Kees, *Het geheim van Oss. Een geschiedenis van de SP* (The Secret of Oss. A History of the Socialist Party), Atlas, Amsterdam.
67. Idem.
68. *Avanta Magazine* no. 12, December 2001.
69. Idem.
70. See note 37.
71. *Trouw*, 27 November 2001.